EBURY PRESS

SMALL WINS EVERY DAY

Luke Coutinho is the lifestyle ambassador and champion for Prime Minister Narendra Modi's Fit India Movement. He has won several national and international awards, and authored four bestsellers.

He practises holistic nutrition and integrative and lifestyle medicine, and is the pioneer of the You Care Wellness Programme, which consults thousands globally. His healing philosophy revolves around cellular nutrition, adequate exercise, quality sleep, emotional wellness and the spirit.

Luke's free content has helped people reverse diabetes, lose fat sustainably, put cancers into remission and overcome suicidal tendencies to live happier lives.

Cancer Care—Aap Ke Liye by Team Luke provides free holistic nutrition and lifestyle support to the underprivileged.

Luke travels globally to speak on holistic wellness, nutrition, disease and more. His ethical wellness platform, You Care Lifestyle, brings products with a farmers-first concept. He is the founder and chief programme mentor for integrative nutrition and dietetics courses at Lifeness Science Institute (LSI).

Celebrating 35 Years of
Penguin Random House India

ADVANCE PRAISE FOR THE BOOK

'An enthusiastic spirit and a happy mind are key signs of well-being, and to lead a happy life you need a multi-pronged approach. Luke Coutinho has helped many with his experience in health and wellness. His ability to inspire people to follow good habits and the right practices is worth emulating. With this book, may he continue to inspire many on the path of wellness. Love and best wishes'—Gurudev Sri Sri Ravi Shankar, The Art of Living

'My dearest Luke,
Small Wins Every Day is such a fabulous collection of all those little daily achievements that make for a successful and happy life. From "mindful eating" to simply "focusing on being a little more active", from "disconnecting from social media" to "connecting inwards with ourselves in simple ways", Luke has curated such useful gems of wisdom that we often tend to ignore or forget. Wishing you loads of success with this one. After all, BIG wins begin with small wins'—Shilpa Shetty Kundra, actress, model, producer, entrepreneur, yoga and fitness enthusiast, author

'Luke has been an integral part of the Fit India Mission since the start, and his approach to celebrating daily victories is refreshing and effective. Wishing him all the best for Small Wins'—Ekta Vishnoi, deputy director general, Sports Authority of India, and mission director, Fit India Mission

'Simple, easy and practical! These are big wins . . . Transformative!'—Mahesh Babu, actor, producer, media personality and philanthropist

'Arianna Huffington, co-founder, and editor-in-chief of the Huffington Post, in her book The Sleep Revolution: Transforming Your life, One Night at a Time, outlines how getting eight hours of sleep every day is your way to finding personal and professional success. In my view, Luke's book Small Wins Every Day is an extension of that concept. This book is a reminder to self that "simple acts" performed for the mind and the body consistently, and from the heart, have the power to make you feel and perform your best. And success and best thinking emanate when you feel your best! Keep practising these suggestions and finding small wins every day!'—Rohit Khanna, managing director, Accenture Strategy and Consulting, New York

'In a world where we are often focused on the big goals, this book reminds us of the importance of celebrating the small wins every day. It helps us understand that progress isn't always linear, and that celebrating the small wins along the way is key to long-term success'—Dr Vinay Deshmane, breast and surgical oncology, P.D. Hinduja Hospital, Breach Candy Hospital and Asian Cancer Institute

'Hi Luke, thank you for thinking of me to be a part of your book. I am highly obliged. This book is so inspiring. My good wishes to you. These are such simple tips which we all know but have been compiled so well together. Continuous improvement is better than delayed perfection. Keep it simple, as Luke puts it. Congratulations for reaching out to so many people via this book'—Udaoy Shah, director, Vishva Group of Companies, Ahmedabad

'Luke's *Small Wins Every Day* is a craftily written, rational and practical book which will guide us towards living a healthier life for a better future. In this fast-paced world of burnouts, Luke shares how small victories, patience and consistency can be game changers. A must-read for everyone!'—Punit K. Goyal, co-founder, BluSmart

SMALL WINS
EVERY DAY

LUKE COUTINHO

EBURY
PRESS

An imprint of Penguin Random House

EBURY PRESS

USA | Canada | UK | Ireland | Australia
New Zealand | India | South Africa | China

Ebury Press is part of the Penguin Random House group of companies
whose addresses can be found at global.penguinrandomhouse.com

Published by Penguin Random House India Pvt. Ltd
4th Floor, Capital Tower 1, MG Road,
Gurugram 122 002, Haryana, India

First published in Ebury Press by Penguin Random House India 2023

10 9 8 7 6 5 4 3 2 1

ISBN 9780143465782

Typeset in Sabon by MAP Systems, Bengaluru, India

www.penguin.co.in

*To my dad for bringing me into this world and
for the many life lessons he taught me. Gratitude not
for a perfect but beautiful life. For teaching me to move
through negativity and be focused on my goal.
For reminding me to use my gift to help those
around me.*

*Tyanna Brooklyn Coutinho—a reminder that
life is beautiful—my family and all of Team Luke,
my patients and fans across the globe.*

Contents

Foreword

'A man with a golden attitude and a healing heart'

These are the words I would use to describe Luke Coutinho (LC). I first met LC during the pandemic at a talk in Dubai, UAE. His talk was very impressive. The impactful yet simple approach by LC was very puzzling to me because here I was sitting in the audience where I felt empowered and optimistic about living a healthier life contrary to my professional experiences. My background and training is in Surgical Medicine, and this approach was very new to me. However, the meeting in Dubai began a beautiful relationship between LC and I.

Small Wins Every Day embodies this philosophy and approach

Writing a book is no easy task, even for authors who write for a living. However, writing a concise book, that is of impact and value and allows the masses to take action is a feat, similar to scaling Everest. I can, for one, attest to this as I write the foreword for this book. This book allows the readers to feel empowered and take action. My personal favourite chapter revolves around breathwork. A practice that we are all aware of and understand that is simple. However, LC, with his magic, makes this already simple practice even simpler in this book, making it one of the most effective practices you will encounter in your healing journey. I use this in my daily life, and I had the privilege to learn other techniques in this book and implement them, for some time now before writing this foreword. This book can do wonders. It is a book you want on your coffee table so you may share this with everyone in your life.

LC, once again, has made this impossible possible because he is *a man with a golden attitude and a healing heart.*

Dr Anirudh Kumar, MD
Surgeon
Cardiovascular—Paediatrics and
Transplantation Medicine
Health Tech Entrepreneur

Why small wins?

Do you know why most people fail to meet their health, lifestyle or body goals? Or why do they fail in love, business, the corporate world or personal growth? There is a beautiful science to this. When you understand this, decide that enough is enough and that it is time for a change, then your life, health, relationships, career and personal growth change for the better.

It all revolves around the beautiful word **DOPAMINE**.

Carelessly used and highly misunderstood, this incredible neurotransmitter is known as the **feel-good** or **reward** molecule. When you achieve a challenging target or win anything that involves difficulty and struggle, for instance, moving from level one to two in a game, you feel a sense of achievement and motivation. This is your dopamine working for you. Dopamine drives, motivates and inspires us to keep going. Without it, one can struggle to stay motivated.

We have all heard of breaking down goals into smaller goals and milestones. As you achieve each of them, they drive you to move forward and achieve the next until you finally hit your main goal. It makes you feel great about yourself.

Let me illustrate this for you. Say you want to be able to do fifty push-ups or ten clean pull-ups or master a complicated yoga asana. On day one, you try to do fifty push-ups and fail. The following day, your muscles are sore. Still, you try to do fifty push-ups, and fail. You are exhausted and in pain. To top it off, your mind starts to create illusions of failure. Your negative self-talk doesn't help. *'I can't do it. It is difficult. I am not strong enough. Maybe I should quit. This is not my cup of tea.'* Your subconscious mind keeps hearing this. You start to burn out and believe that your goal is unrealistic. You lose motivation as you cannot achieve your goal. You do not produce dopamine and cannot feel good.

Similarly, when you enter a new relationship, you set massive goals because you are in love. You want all the good feelings that come with it. You set out to impress, your partner gets impressed, compliments you, loves you back and appreciates you. All of this is good, but then you set unrealistic relationship goals thinking, *the more, the better.* And you can't achieve all of them because your partner also needs space and time and may not be as enthusiastic as you. When you don't meet these goals, you start feeling demotivated, sad and unloved. It marks the beginning of the conflict. You do not produce dopamine or feel good. Your mind begins to tell you that you are failing, unworthy, useless and not meant for love. It stirs up stories and illusions that get out of control.

When you set unrealistic goals and keep failing, your intelligently designed brain tries to protect you from the pain and negative emotions that come with failure. It tells you, *'Don't perform this again because you will fail.'* It creates neural patterns over time when you fail, and negative thoughts follow.

How do we change these limiting thought patterns? By creating new ones. We do this by breaking down your goals into smaller goals that still hold some challenges but are ones that you can achieve over time. As you do, you produce more dopamine, feel good and start to be driven to activate the next goal leading to the larger goal you created.

A study that analysed 12,000 diary entries of 238 employees across seven companies found that capturing little wins enhanced motivation and boosted self-confidence. These simple changes can trigger a positive chain reaction. When stacked over time, these contributed to significant successes and happiness.

The secret is to keep the smaller goals challenging because if a goal is too easy, you will produce little or no dopamine.

This is what *Small Wins Every Day* is all about. We break down our life, health, love and career goals into small wins that we achieve every day and then move on to the next and then the next small goal. In this process of consistency beautifully coupled with self-discipline, we begin to achieve the main goals we desire.

We learn to achieve and celebrate small wins and use that dopamine to drive, inspire and motivate us to move to the next goal. This journey continues until we achieve the main goal.

What my experience has taught me

In my practice of integrative and lifestyle medicine for over nine years now, I have observed one or two commonalities in patients who get better, recover from deadly conditions, reverse lifestyle diseases, lose or gain weight the right way, or improve cognitive health, relationships and happiness at workplaces and have solid personal growth. These are consistency and self-discipline. Right now, if you are failing somewhere—be it in your health, relationships, workplace, business or simply in life, it is because you have become inconsistent with the small actions that matter. Self-discipline is never a rigid process, it allows for failure, but you need to get back on track as quickly as possible. Consistency doesn't mean you will not fail. It means that when you do, you get back to the consistency of those required actions in every aspect of your life. Hence, small wins practised with consistency and self-disciple can yield the biggest results of all. We need to shift our focus from complication to simplicity because simplicity is the new luxury. It is in simplicity that we find peace, freedom, joy and great health in all ways.

Welcome to Small Wins Every Day

I was inspired to write this book because we have launched and successfully run these small wins across the globe through our social media handles for years. We have had close to 10,000 people on Telegram alone and over a million followers on our other platforms engage in these small wins. The testimonials that have poured in are nothing short of spectacular. This tried and tested model has helped thousands transform their lives, and it is now your turn to do the same.

There is one simple rule. If you fail, just start again. You miss a day, start again tomorrow. If you feel demotivated, it is all right for today. But tomorrow we get back on track. Remember, things and people may get difficult in life, but difficult doesn't mean impossible.

The foundation of every small win in this book is simplicity. In a world full of complexity, simplicity is a luxury we should all aim for. From cancer patients to those suffering from diabetes and even Alzheimer's, if there is one approach that has worked, it is the simple principle of keeping the fundamentals in place. The biggest gap that exists today is not a lack of knowledge but the confusion caused by surplus knowledge. Over and above this, there is a lack of action, discipline and consistency.

With these small wins, take one step at a time, excel at it, then move to the next and begin to turn all of them into a lifestyle. We want everyone reading this book to use it and make a difference in their lives. Once done, carry it forward to someone in your family, to friends, relatives, or even society. Be an accountability buddy for someone.

We have been running challenges around the world for years. And millions of people have joined and transformed their lives with them. You can be a part of this small army too.

Begin your journey with these 100 wins, one day at a time.

With love and gratitude,
Luke Coutinho

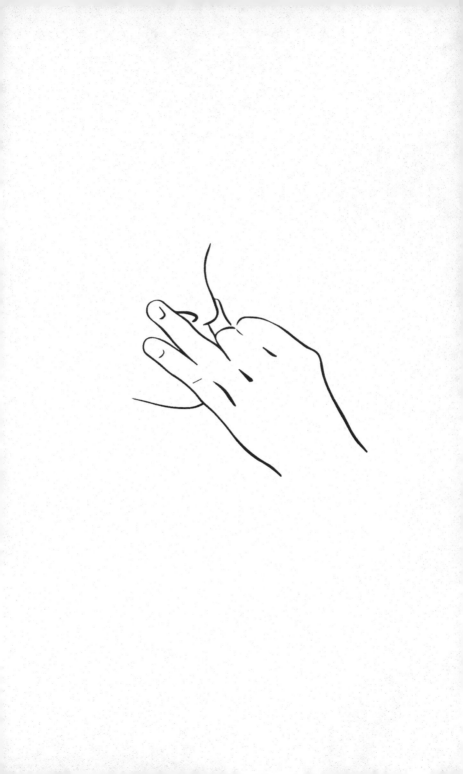

Three minutes of anulom vilom

Prana or breath is the force of life. Today we will practise three minutes of anulom vilom pranayama. Also known as alternate nostril breathing, it helps balance the energy within us. In hatha yoga, anulom translates to going with the grain, and vilom translates to going against the grain.

Make the ancient practice of anulom vilom a lifestyle. Do this every day, in the morning on waking up and before you drift off to sleep at night. Feel how it transforms you over time in different ways. Deep breathing or pranayama infuses a tremendous amount of energy and life force into trillions of cells at a body and mind level. There is tremendous power and medicine in your breath when used well. All it takes is three minutes. Do this with discipline and consistency.

How to do it

1. Sit in padmasana. Keep your spine straight. Centre yourself.

2. Fold the middle and index fingers of your right hand. Bring them close to your nose.

3. Place your thumb on the right nostril and the ring finger on your left nostril.

4. Close the right nostril with your thumb and start slowly and mindfully inhaling oxygen through your left nostril.

5. Once your lungs are full of air, close your left nostril with the ring finger. Keep the right nostril closed as you do this. Now try holding your breath for a few seconds.

6. Now remove your thumb from the right nostril and exhale slowly through it. Don't lose focus of your breath.

7. Repeat the same process by inhaling from your right nostril and exhaling through the left.

8. Repeat this cycle for three minutes.

Master the art of chewing

Today we will focus on slowing down when eating and mastering the art of chewing. Ask yourself: *How often do I take the time to truly savour every bite I eat?* Remember, digestion begins in the mouth where the enzymes amylase and lipase in your saliva start breaking down food when you chew. When you eat your food too quickly, you fail to use your teeth to break down the food into smaller particles and send larger chunks of food into your stomach. This leads to our stomach producing excess acid and enzymes, causes irritation of your gut lining and paves the way for acidity, bloating and indigestion. Chew well to reduce the load on your digestive system.

How to do it

1. Keep your mealtime a gadget-free zone.
2. When you sit down to eat, bless your food and express gratitude. This can change the energy of the food.
3. Take six deep breaths to move from the sympathetic nervous system to a parasympathetic state.
4. Start eating one bite at a time.
5. Chew every morsel so well that it becomes pasty enough to swallow and then take the next bite. Do NOT rush. Be mindful of when to stop eating.
6. Practise, practise, practise—until it becomes a ritual and habit.

Wait! There's broccoli stuck in your teeth!

Today, focus on rinsing your mouth with water after every meal. This is essential for dental health and the oral microbiome. Swish the water in your mouth for a few seconds and spit it out. You will be surprised to see small bits of food particles that could have stayed stuck in between your teeth!

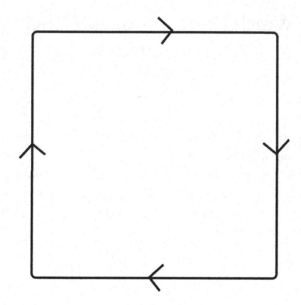

Box breathing

Today, we will focus on a beautiful breathing technique called box breathing. Whether you are looking for relaxation, focus, sleep or calm, this breathing technique will help you.

How to do it

1. Sit in a comfortable posture, keep your back straight and shoulders rolled backward.
2. Next, inhale through your nostrils for four seconds.
3. Then, hold the breath for another four seconds.
4. Now, slowly exhale through your nostrils for four seconds.
5. Finally, hold the exhaled breath for four seconds before you start the next inhale.
6. Repeat this six or more times.

This breathing is in the 4:4:4:4 ratio (four counts inhale, four counts hold, four counts exhale and four counts hold). However, you could also try 5:5:5:5 or 6:6:6:6, whatever feels comfortable.

'Given the fast pace of our lives and living in a time that we are so switched on or perpetually wired, switching off and relaxing are not luxuries. These are NECESSITIES.'

Pre-bedtime gadget detox

Today, one hour before bedtime, switch off all your gadgets, whether it is your phone, iPad or television. If one hour seems like a big challenge, start small. Try thirty minutes. Plan what you want to do in those gadget-free thirty minutes or one hour. Build yourself a solid night-time routine.

Solve crossword puzzles, play sudoku, have pleasant conversations with family members, try left nostril breathing, 4–7–8 breathing or even bee breathing. Read your favourite book, write in your journal, meditate, set intentions for the following day, take a warm shower, make love or practise yoga nidra or savasana. Try to do this for a couple of days and see how the quality of your sleep transforms.

Want to feel good about yourself in under three minutes? Just BRG

This simple **BRG exercise** that I designed stands for **Be, Receive** and **Give thanks**. Do this before going to bed at night. It allows you to count the little, simple and inexpensive blessings you often take for granted.

- **B** stands for **to be**. Learn to just 'be'. In a world where you are constantly trying to fit in, changing one mask after another, you need to take a minute out of your schedule and be you. Don't do anything. Just sit back and be one with yourself. Take a couple of deep breaths to recentre yourself, if it helps.
- **R** stands for **receive**. Go over the little things you have received from the moment you woke up in the morning. It could be a cup of perfectly brewed chai or a hug from your loved one. Every little thing you receive counts.

- **G** stands for **giving thanks**. Once you have acknowledged everything you have received, offer gratitude. Give thanks straight from your heart.

'Hold close to you, very close to you, what's important and meaningful—family, kids, real friends, parents. Life is short and uncertain, yet beautiful whilst we cherish what we have. Nothing is permanent but enjoy it all in the now. Don't postpone it.'

Are you feeling unhappy or low? Try this one-minute meditation

I call this the loving figure meditation. All you need to do is sit, close your eyes and think of someone you love or someone who loves you. This person must be someone whose mere thought warms your heart. They could be alive or no longer with you—it doesn't matter. As you start thinking of that person, you will feel a change of emotions in your heart.

Imagine the person walking towards you. It could be a child or an adult. They smile, sit by your side, put their arms around you and hold you close. I want you to be in that embrace, be in that warmth and experience that magic. Some of you may shed tears, but what you will be left feeling is intense love.

Have a good cry today

Crying is cathartic. It is often misunderstood as a sign of weakness and vulnerability. But even science says **crying is good for you**. It releases your stress hormones, promotes relaxation, alleviates pain, brings emotional balance and helps you sleep better. Your small win for today is to have a good cry.

If you feel genuine pain, cry to process it and let it reach its natural death. If you don't want anyone to see you crying, lock yourself in a room and cry in privacy. If it makes you feel better, cry in front of a close friend. Understand that it is a mechanism built in us to help us survive and adapt to changing environments. A hurtful event might have occurred a long while ago, but if it is still pulling you back, you need to process those emotions, face them head-on and cry it out once and for all. It is okay to feel every emotion rather than holding everything inside or putting up a façade, which can get overwhelming and confusing.

Get dirty

Start playing with pure and organic mud. Ensure you do not use mud that is contaminated by animal urine or poop. Playing with mud can help improve one's gut health, especially that of children. If you do not have access to a garden, order organic mud online and create a mud pit. When my daughter was growing up, I got a large box and filled it with soil so she could play with it every day. Good microbes get stuck under your nails and enter your system and feed your gut microbiome with perfect nutrition. They repopulate it. Remember how as children we often played with mud and came home dirty and dusty? Many of us don't allow our kids to do that today. It is time to go back to the basics. Try this with your kids, even if it is for just five or ten minutes a day. It is peaceful and almost meditative in a way. Do this mindfully.

A healthy dose of vitamin sunshine

When you wake up today, allow your body to soak in some sunshine. While we have known this for decades, there is a great deal of fear in people today about the sun and its connection with cancer. We prescribe sunlight to our patients and the outcomes of soaking in some sunshine daily are amazing. It improves your mood, energy and sleep. The sun is life after all. There would be no life or organism alive without the sun. No human or machine is superior to the intelligence of nature. However, keep in mind that the sun and ultraviolet rays can be harmful when overdone. So, start with soaking in the sun for as little as ten minutes and gradually build it up to fifteen or twenty minutes. It is preferable to get the morning or late evening sunshine. Avoid sitting in the sun when it is at its peak. That is harsh and can burn your skin.

Besides increasing your vitamin D3 levels (which again plays a role in mood regulation), the sun exposes us to powerful infrared rays that lower inflammation, regulate sleep patterns, elevate mood by releasing serotonin (the happy hormone) and produce cellular melatonin, which is one of the most powerful antioxidants. Low levels of serotonin and melatonin are associated with every single mood disorder known today. If you are living in a cold country, use an infrared lamp instead. Be careful if you have an existing skin issue or have been medically advised to avoid infrared rays.

BTSTS
(breathe, touch, smell, taste, see)

Feeling anxious? Here's a simple and powerful exercise for you.

Pause and slow down your inhales and exhales. Now, look around you and find something you can touch. Next, try and focus on any one smell around you. Then, try and feel what taste you have in your mouth. Lastly, look around and try to focus on anything that you can look at or see for a few moments.

This is **B**reathe **T**ouch **S**mell **T**aste **S**ee.

It is a type of focused distraction that can break the chain of unwanted thoughts in your mind.

This simple exercise has worked for hundreds of our patients struggling with anxiety. You may be saying to yourself, '*This is too much to do especially when I'm feeling anxious*', but my question to you is—What are you doing to feel better? Any progress in life requires action, effort and work. That's how you move from where you are stuck to progress. You lose nothing by trying. Chronic anxiety causes disease, disharmony and suffering, and there is always something you can do to feel better.

Write a letter to the universe

This may sound airy fairy, but I am asking you to try this once with awe and wonder if you never have. Keep no fear and disbelief because you lose nothing by trying. When you do this, it aligns your deepest desires with your heart and mind.

I share this not because I read it in a book but because I have read it in several of them, practised it with faith, belief and awe, and today most of my life is built on visualization and manifestation. The good and the bad. Bad? Yes, because we can even manifest the bad when our thoughts and spirit are not aligned with the authentic self. It is like a nocebo, where negative self-talk can become your experience and reality. However, coming to the good, I am grateful and blessed that the majority of my life is based on what I have visualized with patience and faith. And if something hasn't happened for me yet, it is because it was not meant to happen or it is not the right time yet. It could be a person, thing, event, money or anything else.

Write that letter. Simply visualize your best life and then start writing with no limits and fear. Feel how it will be when you get what you ask for. Once done, gracefully surrender the outcome. Don't try to micromanage it, get negative or impatient. Surrender and get back to life and your work.

'Fear will never allow you to enjoy what you have in your life. All the abundance, goodness, and material things that you may have, these will bring you no joy when you live from a space of fear, love from a space of fear, decide from a space of fear, or choose or speak from a space of fear. Overcome fear. It is on the other side of fear that exists joy, happiness, peace and meaning.'

Walk the talk

Need a vitamin for good health that is free? Try **vitamin W**. This isn't a pill you can pop, but an inexpensive everyday lifestyle change you can adopt. Vitamin W stands for walking.

What are its benefits?

- Walking is free.
- You can walk anytime and anywhere (of course, subject to the weather).
- Whether you are in your thirties, forties, fifties or even eighties, you can walk if you are physically able.

Who says you need to begin with one-hour power walks? Start small.

Today, focus on going for a ten-minute gentle walk after every meal. Schedule your calls for this duration if you can or listen to a song or two. Get that walk after your meals, no matter where you are. Practise this with discipline and consistency.

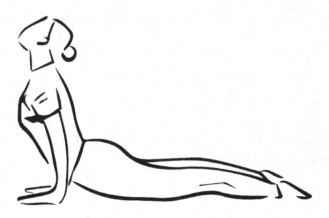

Salute the sun

Practise three surya namaskars with grace, coordinated breath and movement. Surya namaskars, or sun salutations, were practised thousands of years ago by saints to worship the sun.

Known as 'the ultimate asana', it has physical, emotional and spiritual benefits. It improves flexibility and strength, calms your mind and activates the blocked chakras of the body. With a combination of eight asanas and a repetition of four of them (twelve asanas) in one set, surya namaskar engages almost 92 per cent of your body's muscles from head to toe. Do this in the morning. If you don't know how to do this, try to learn and perfect this beautiful full-body movement.

How to do it

1. **Pranamasana:** This prayer pose makes steps 1 and 12. It calms the mind, nervous system and body and balances the heart chakra.

2. **Hasta uttanasana:** The raised arms pose makes steps 2 and 11. It improves flexibility, reduces back pain, strengthens the spine and releases tension around the neck muscles. It expands the lungs and balances the throat chakra.

3. **Hasta padasana:** The standing forward bend makes steps 3 and 10. It strengthens the back, abdominal muscles and nervous system. It also stretches the calf and glute muscles and increases blood flow to the brain to improve memory and focus. It aids digestion by increasing blood flow to the abdomen and balances the solar plexus chakra.

4. **Ashwa sanchalanasana:** Also known as the equestrian pose, it makes for steps 4 and 9. It increases flexibility in your legs and stretches your spine, quadriceps and hip muscles. It helps to balance the heart, third eye and solar plexus chakras.

5. **Phalakasana:** The shoulder plank pose is step 5. It will tone your wrists and legs, and build arm muscles. It puts pressure on the core muscles and is excellent for reducing belly fat. It enhances your posture by aligning your back muscles and spine. It activates the solar plexus chakra.

6. **Ashtanga namaskar:** This eight-limbed pose is step 6. It strengthens your chest, arms and legs. It is beneficial for the lower abdominal organs and balances the sacral, root and solar plexus chakras.

7. **Bhujangasana:** The cobra pose is step 7. It alleviates headaches and backache by relieving tension

in your neck, back and spine. It promotes your spine's flexibility and improves posture, thus reducing the chance of slipped discs. It helps in balancing the sacral chakra.

8. **Adho mukha svanasana:** This downward-facing dog pose is step 8. It lowers stress, improves blood circulation, enhances respiration and aids better posture. It makes your arms and legs stronger and relieves varicose veins. It also stretches your calf and spine muscles and is known to activate the sacral chakra.

Eat a crucifer today for your DNA

Are you eating your cruciferous veggies? Try to cook and eat at least one cruciferous vegetable today and on most days, if not every day. What are some examples of these? Broccoli, cauliflower, cabbage, kale, garden cress, bok choy, Brussels sprouts, mustard greens, arugula, collard greens, Swiss chard and so on.

These help with deep cellular nutrition and work for your immunity and DNA. They contain glucosinolates, which have anti-inflammatory and antioxidant properties and can create cell apoptosis (cell death) and stop tumour growth. High in fibre, protein, vitamins and minerals, crucifers boost heart health, reduce bad cholesterol, lower blood pressure and decrease the risk of obesity and diabetes.

Four-minute Tabata

What is Tabata? It is a high-intensity interval training that works to increase your heart rate rapidly and burn as many calories as you can in a short amount of time. Designed by Dr Izumi Tabata in 1996, this workout can stretch for anywhere between four to twenty minutes. We will begin with a four-minute Tabata training.

This will help boost your metabolism, take less than five minutes and will help you build lean muscle. It may include movements such as squats, crunches, burpees, mountain climbers, push-ups and lunges.

How to do it?

- Download a free Tabata app on your phone today.
- Select your favourite bodyweight or aerobic exercise.
- Now do the exercise for twenty seconds and then rest for ten seconds.

- Do this with discipline and consistency for the next four minutes.
- Choose your level of intensity based on what suits you.
- Don't overdo it. Give it your best shot.

Sitting is the new smoking: Did you move today?

Your intelligently designed body was never designed to sit for long hours. Every forty-five minutes to an hour, stand up and stretch. Try to touch your toes. Get up and walk around the room to get that glass of water. We win by not sitting continuously. It is always the simple things that make a huge difference.

Did you get your dose of vitamin I?

Vitamin I is not a pill you can pop or medicine you can inject. It stands for intention. Set your intentions for today. Whether it is the tasks you want to accomplish, the calls you need to close, that one meal you want to get right, a ten-minute walk in nature or spending time with your family, set your intentions. Your intentions are invisible guiding threads that get you through your day with purpose. Do this mindfully.

Imbibing the attitude of gratitude

Today, we will start the practice of deepening gratitude by starting a gratitude journal. When you wake up, take a deep breath. Gently reflect on and write down three people, things or events you are grateful for. It does not matter how big or small. Once you have written them down, read them mindfully. Feel every word in your mind and heart. Notice how kick-starting your day with the attitude of gratitude changes it.

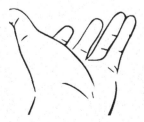

A simple act of kindness

Focus mindfully on doing one or more random acts of kindness today. It could be something as simple as making someone a cup of tea, helping your colleague with a task they have been struggling with, feeding a stray or making a call to a loved one and reminding them how important they are to you. Don't do it with any expectations, just straight from the heart. These little acts of kindness and the satisfaction they bring can benefit your health at all levels. You will feel good at a spiritual level, especially in times when you feel low and disconnected. This practice will help you vibrate at a higher level. Make a difference in someone's life. It is not always about donating money. It could be the smallest gesture—a smile, a thought or an intention for somebody else.

Eat the rainbow

Your gut is the epicentre of your health. The more colours you can add to your plate, the more diversity there will be in your gut microbiome. Today, focus on eating a rainbow meal where you add different colours and food groups to create a balanced meal including nuts, fruits, veggies, seeds, lentils, legumes, whole grains and so on. Do this well.

- The largest portion will consist of vegetables (starchy and non-starchy)—50 per cent.
- The second largest portion will consist of proteins (animal or plant-based)—25 to 35 per cent.
- The smallest portion will consist of carbohydrates (grains and cereals)—15 to 25 per cent.

Try to follow this rule for all meals—breakfast, lunch and dinner. Just reduce the portions for dinner.

Please note: The percentage of each portion may vary based on your body requirements, medical condition, weight goals and so on. Keep your healthcare professional or integrative nutritionist in the loop.

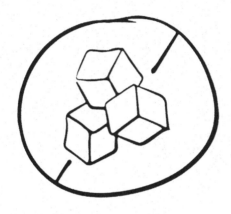

Say bye-bye to sugar for the next three days!

Your challenge is to say no to sugar and its many disguises. For the next seventy-two hours, practise restraint mindfully. No refined sugar, jaggery, brown sugar, coconut sugar, agave syrup or any products that contain them. The temptation might be real. The challenge may seem daunting, but I believe in YOU. It is not impossible.

You will not only build stronger resilience towards temptation but also experience improved gut and oral health. Watch how avoiding sugar stabilizes your energy levels and curbs acidity, brain fog, energy crash, irritability and mood swings. Read food labels carefully and encourage a loved one to join you in this challenge as an accountability buddy. Experience its magic and build a healthier relationship with food.

'*Excessive convenience, instant gratification, a feeling of constant entitlement and inflated egos are all the curse and downfall of most humans today. Slow down and adopt the pace of nature—if you don't, life and your body will find ways to slow you down eventually. Put in the sacrifice and effort. Complaining, blaming and labelling yourself depressed won't get you anywhere.*'

Disconnect to reconnect with nature

Your mornings are sacred. How you spend that first hour after waking up can set the foundation and the tone for how the rest of your day will unfold. This is why waking up to a disturbing email or news can have a ripple effect on the rest of your day. Don't wake up to information and notifications bombarding you. After waking up, do not switch on your phone for at least one hour. What can you do instead? Use that time to open your window and connect with the natural light. Look at the sky, trees, nature or sunrise for at least ten minutes to align your circadian rhythm. This helps create a healthy sleep cycle. So, nature first, phones and gadgets later, friends!

Are you making your Sundays meaningful?

Is it Sunday yet? Practise gadget and social media fasting today. Move from the virtual world and thrive in the real world. Reminisce over memories that spark joy, spend time in nature, rest and recharge for the week ahead. Take the time to make an appreciation and gratitude list if you can. Feel what you write deeply, and say this to yourself before you retire for the night: 'What an amazing day this has been. I feel good!'

Don't be a couch potato

If you are sitting for long hours watching TV, surfing your gadgets, bingeing on movies and shows or consuming content, try to take a break every thirty to forty-five minutes. Get up from your seat or couch and walk around the house. Do ten jumping jacks or five squats, or try a one-minute plank. Break the sitting.

'You have time for social media but you don't have time to slowly eat your meal, invest in some movement, sleep or emotional wellness. Your priorities are wrong and you surely have time management and planning issues. Fix it.'

Try LSD, it's legal!

When you master control over LSD, that's where the magic begins. It has zero side effects. This alone won't heal but creates an environment within your body that is healing for you. Before you mistake LSD for an illegal drug, let me tell you that I am referring to Long Slow Deep breaths. This is the art of slowing down your breath—inhale and exhale. And then increasing the retention of the end of your inhale and the beginning of your exhale. And the retention between the end of your exhale and the beginning of your next inhale.

Give your heart a little warmth

Today we focus on three memories that bring a smile to your face and kindle a warm feeling in your heart. Think deeply about these. Play these memories in your mind and focus on every detail. Relive those moments as much as possible. Once done, write them down. Now hold this piece of paper or book close to your heart. Every time you feel low or negative thoughts cloud your mind, revisit these powerful memories on paper. Feel the shift this creates.

Let your guard down

Today I want you to practise winning by mastering the art of flowing, which refers to embracing change. It is not difficult. It is easy. All you need to do is mindfully stop resisting one thing you have been doing for the longest time. Is it a person or a task? You make that choice. Let your guard down and face today by confronting it. Confrontation doesn't always mean having an argument or being aggressive. There is immense power in acceptance and letting go too. Sit down and carefully reflect. How is this person or task affecting you? What is stopping you? Is there anything within your power to resolve the emotions it is causing? If there is, act respectfully on it. If not, let it flow, let it go and accept. When you do not resist, see where the mind takes you. Do this well.

Eat without guilt

Today, we practise eating without guilt. How many times have you looked at your favourite meal and calculated how many calories it will add and how many hours you will have to work out to burn it off? Guilt is a negative emotion. If you are going to eat that bowl of ice cream, burger or pizza, do it because you want to enjoy it. Create an environment of happiness because every emotion you feel influences how your body accepts and breaks this food down. Trillions of your cells vibrate with the emotions you feel. If you are going to eat with guilt and overthink it, don't eat it at all. If you think you will genuinely enjoy what you desire to eat, bless and consume it with gratitude and love.

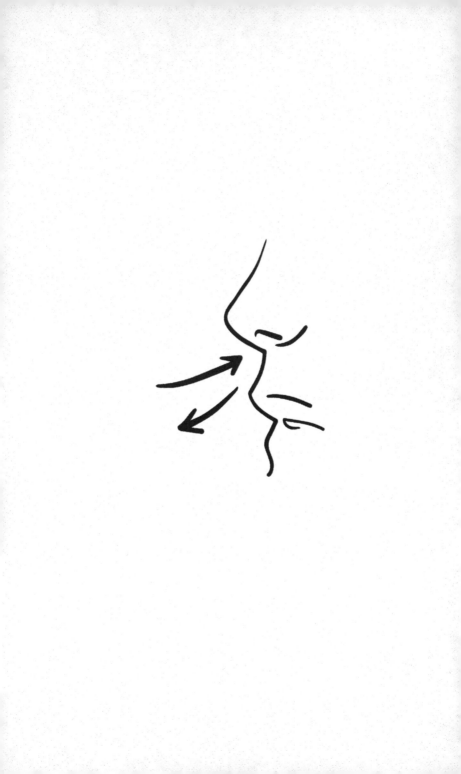

Vitamin O for breakfast, lunch and dinner

This vitamin is freely and abundantly available. You don't have to pay a single penny for it. Vitamin O stands for oxygen. Today, we focus on taking three long, slow and deep breaths before and after every meal.

Here's a simple exercise:

- Before you start your meal, take three deep breaths to flood your body and stomach with oxygen.
- Inculcate a method of mindful eating.
- With every bite that you take, try to get into the habit of taking a deep breath. One inhale and one exhale.
- Every time you inhale oxygen, you help your body balance its acidic and alkaline levels naturally.
- Once you have ended your meal, repeat the three long, slow and deep breaths.

Are you soakin' those raisins?

This powerful practice has existed in our country for centuries and can be a simple yet impactful lifestyle change you can make. All you need to do is take six black raisins and soak them overnight. Wake up the following morning and have these on an empty stomach. Throw the water out. Do not drink it. When you soak dried black raisins, two things happen. You wash off any dirt on the raisin, and you enhance the bioavailability of its nutrients and antioxidants. This simple practice can ease your bowel movements, curb cravings, help manage blood pressure, improve sleep, boost oral hygiene, promote glowing skin and hair, and even boost immunity and energy levels.

'To be accepted, first learn to accept yourself.
To be loved, first learn to love yourself.
To be able to forgive, first learn to forgive yourself.
The kingdom of heaven is within you.
The kingdom of hell is also within you.
It is what you make of your thoughts, feelings,
emotions and perceptions, and how attached
you stay to them.
Let go sometimes for your peace of mind and
the heaven within.'

There is somebody you need to thank today: Your body!

When was the last time you took a minute from your day to reflect on your beautifully and intelligently designed body? Most of us spend every waking minute finding faults in our appearance. Too fat, too thin, too tall, too short, no abs, thunder thighs and so on. But do we take the time to recognize that every second of every day and night our extraordinary body works to keep us thriving? Remember this and pause in deep gratitude. Whisper a thank you straight from the heart. Practise this and live with awareness no matter what goes on in your life.

Finite time, infinite possibilities

A lesson I have learnt over the last decade of my practice with terminally-ill people and those suffering from physical and mental ailments is that we think we are in control. But the truth is we are not for most things. The more we try to control what cannot be, the more stress, anxiety, burnout, guilt and resentment we invite into our lives. Your exercise for today is to list what you think is within your control and what isn't. Look at this list and reflect on it deeply. Remind yourself every day that your time is finite. Knowing this, reflect on the changes you are willing to make to live a more abundant life. What isn't within your control, accept and let it go. Do this well.

'People's opinions are the worst way for you to determine how you feel about yourself. If you allow this to keep happening, these people will own you because they own your emotions. Other people's perception of you is none of your business. You've got to move on, living your truth and being you.'

Own your narrative

It is astonishing how most of us live in fear and anxiety because we make other people's stories our own. It does not have to be this way. Your creations come from the thoughts, belief patterns and things that you give the most energy to. You can either manifest good health or disease. You can manifest love or block it out of your life. You can either manifest your world or destroy it by how much energy and desire you put into those thoughts. Decide what deserves your heart and mind space today. Write it down if you must. Nobody can be positive all the time. But it is with consistent mindfulness practice that when we start feeling negative, we can learn to gently shift our energy to the thoughts we should be nurturing. Don't believe in being positive all the time. It is okay to feel sadness, envy, anger, guilt and so on. But how quickly you shift your energy from those negative thoughts to what you have and want is where your magic lies. You are the main character of your story. Own your narrative.

'Stop compounding your suffering with your self-judgment all the time. Perfectionism isn't a goal! Aim for excellence over being a perfectionist—the stress and anxiety will be less.'

It's self-care-o-clock

Who are you? This may seem like a big and loaded question. But it all starts with the way you think about and perceive yourself. Do you know who you are? Or are you waiting for society and the people around you to define you? While we all have strengths and areas of opportunity, life is about building on those areas of opportunity and optimizing those strengths. Many of us stop using our strengths because we are too focused on our weaknesses.

Every morning remind yourself of who you are and how great you are in many beautiful ways. Take your notepad and list five qualities or traits you love about yourself. Read them out loud. The next time self-doubt clouds your mind and judgement, revisit this note. Watch how your perception transforms. The power lies in mindfully choosing and nurturing thoughts that energetically drive you.

Five-minute meditation, but keep it unrestrained

You can practise this in the little pockets of time or breaks you get during the day. Meditation does not have to be complicated. It is easy. This one only needs five minutes of your time. Set a timer, sit with your back straight, eyes gently closed, and follow your inhale and exhale. As you do this, let thoughts come and go. Don't try to stop them. Try to recentre yourself. Practise. Practise. And practise until you master it. This meditation is particularly effective when done first thing in the morning upon waking up and before you slip into bed.

Imagine the best

Your exercise for today is simple. It is not about training your mind but retraining your mind. Try to think consciously about what you want rather than focusing on what you don't want. The more you mindfully do this, the better most aspects of your life get. Imagine the best always. After all, we don't get anything out of imagining the worst. Think and imagine the best. Write it down with conviction and belief. Once you have done this, surrender.

'How many of you can say you have had a good day or you feel good at the end of your day? On most days, if not every day, that's the measure of the quality of your life. You may have had ups and downs, that's normal. But feeling good despite everything—now that's rich.'

Feel your feelings

It is not your job to be happy all the time. Nor is it to be at peace 24x7. Your job is to return to a state of happiness and peace when life keeps throwing you curveballs and off your path. Believe it or not, it will happen to you, your children, your parents or other loved ones. But it doesn't mean that life is unfair. It is just another reason for us to invest in ourselves. Self-work, mindfulness, meditation, learning the power of acceptance and letting go are crucial. So if you are feeling certain negative feelings today, feel them. But bring yourself back to a state of peace and happiness.

Want a natural gut cleanse?
Try this

Prebiotics and probiotics are great for your gut health, but did you know that nature has built the unique intelligence within each of us to clean out the gut and repopulate the microflora on its own? I am speaking about the power of fasting.

- Fast mindfully today; do it scientifically.
- Do not starve or bracket yourself in 16:8 fasting windows.
- Do what is natural to you.
- Do not push your body until it is acidic to reach a magic number.
- Break your fast with a glass of water and a few soaked nuts, followed by fruits.

Use this inner physician well. It doesn't cost you a penny.

Have you tried moon breathing?

Try this simple breathing technique before bed. Your left nostril (chandra nadi) corresponds to the moon. It is known to soothe the mind and body. Left nostril breathing, also known as moon breathing or chandra bhedana, helps you instantly relax and cool down, a prerequisite for deep sleep. It is also said to deepen mindfulness, promote compassion and stability, and stimulate the parasympathetic nervous system.

How to do it

- Sit cross-legged on the bed or floor. You can even use a chair.
- Keep your back straight, chin parallel to the ground and shoulders slightly rolled back.
- Make a pranayama mudra with your right hand by pressing the index and middle finger toward the base of your thumb. This is the Vishnu mudra.
- Now, use your right thumb to shut the right nostril.

- Inhale through your left nostril while keeping the right one closed.
- After a full inhale, close your left nostril and exhale through the right nostril. It comprises one round.
- Now, close your right nostril and inhale through your left nostril again.
- Practise ten, fifteen, twenty or twenty-five rounds of this breathing just before you sleep.
- Keep your eyes closed to enter a state of deep relaxation. Do this well.

'There is:
No perfect relationship
No perfect job
No perfect parent
No perfect kid
No perfect friend
No perfect body
No perfect life
And that's why there is beauty and
peace in cultivating
Tolerance
Acceptance
Forgiveness
Letting go
Understanding
Compassion
Do this if you want true freedom, peace, and joy.'

Fake it till you make it

Can you trick your brain to feel happy? The answer is a big YES. How? By faking a smile. You may know the difference between a forced and genuine smile, but science says your body cannot distinguish the difference between the two. No matter how you are feeling today, get those facial muscles moving and force a smile. This simple act can release that dopamine and serotonin, instantly lift your mood, alleviating stress and maybe even increasing longevity. Do this well.

How do you flow into a space of receiving?

Most of us are in a state of the constant pursuit of getting, but when we move to a space of receiving, the energy changes and aligns with what we truly desire. The secret to receiving is allowing yourself to surrender without expectations of what you must receive. To be in the energy of allowing and receiving unconditional abundance. You can never receive if you feel unworthy of receiving what you want. Remove the conditions, let go of the past, the baggage you carry and the fear of the future, and be open to receiving. Know that receiving requires no physical exertion, only intention and allowing.

Affirm this with faith and belief, and from the depth of your heart today and every day.

I am receiving guidance.
I am receiving safety.
I am receiving protection.
I am receiving great help.

96

I am receiving love.
I am receiving abundance.
Yes, I am receiving all this and more, and everything is
perfect at this moment. Thank you for this moment.

When you are in a state of flow, you receive beautifully. In a state of blame, complaints, whining, constant fear and anxiety, anger, guilt, resentment or envy, you can never flow or receive. When you receive something, you want to feel fulfilled and abundant. So, do this well.

What are your final thoughts before you hit the hay?

Your final thoughts before sleeping matter. Want to sleep deeper tonight? Try this. As you lay your head down, close your eyes and think of all the times you helped or served someone and felt good about yourself. Hold that warm feeling of joy in your heart and surrender yourself to deep and beautiful sleep.

This has worked beautifully not just for me but for thousands of our clients. If it works for you, great. If it doesn't, at least you felt good. Isn't that nice? Sleep well tonight.

'If you hang on to something of the past that gives you suffering, every time you relive it in your mind, you get the same suffering over and over again. This will create a cycle of suffering for you that gets stronger each time. LET GO.'

It is time to surrender

Today's exercise is simple. I want you to reflect deeply on three problems you have been struggling with. Write them down on a piece of paper. Once you have done this, close your eyes, hold that sheet of paper close and ask or pray for help and guidance in overcoming these problems. Are you done? Now comes the most crucial part: gracefully surrender. Detach yourself from the outcome. Watch how this creates a shift in you and helps you experience a feeling of lightness. Do this straight from the heart. It is a small win but a beautiful practice. Even if you are sceptical about its effectiveness, you lose nothing by trying. Do this today. Keep winning.

Pull it up

Your ability to do a pull-up defines your level of strength and fitness. The best investment you can make right now is to get a pull-up bar and master a basic pull-up. If you cannot do a pull-up, begin by simply hanging from the bar to strengthen your back and arms. Apply variations here as well, like chin-ups, close-handed and wide-handed grips, among others. As you develop strength, you can even strap on additional weight such as a weighted vest. No other weight training exercise engages as many muscles at a single time than a pull-up does, and that is why it is difficult at first.

Some people have never even stepped into a gym but do pull-ups and have chiselled, ripped and lean bodies. While this may not necessarily be your goal, pull-ups work for body toning, boosting metabolism and fat loss. There are ample variations for beginners like a supported pull-up. Make it a part of your lifestyle!

Make your timetable:
Run your day like a boss

Grab a notepad and pen and get down to budgeting your time for the various activities you want to accomplish through the day. The biggest roadblock for most people is their lack of organization. It is the number one cause for a day spiralling out of your hands. While making this timetable, do not forget to allocate time for yourself. The timetable will also help you prioritize what is important and put what isn't on the back burner. Once you ace it, you will start running your day instead of your day running you. Look at it like this. Take eight hours from the twenty-four hours of the day for sleep, and make it non-negotiable. Plan the rest of your activities in the remaining eighteen hours. This may include work, me-time, family time, workouts, socializing and so on. Run your day like a boss.

Juice the rainbow

This is one of the simplest yet most powerful, multipurpose, nutritious and cleansing rainbow juices, and you can make it at home. Do this if it suits you. If you are allergic to any of these ingredients, avoid them. If you have a medical condition with dietary restrictions, check with your healthcare provider before trying this out.

- Carrot (carotenoids and falcarinol)
- Beetroot (nitrate-rich, high in fibre and digestive enzymes)
- Lemon (ascorbic acid, i.e., vitamin C)
- Cucumber (90 per cent water, vitamins A, B, K and C, electrolytes, polyphenols)
- A dash of virgin olive oil (healthy fats)
- A dash of black pepper (antioxidants such as piperine and the subtle heat you need)
- Blend and consume with the rich fibre.
- If you find it too thick to drink, strain and sip.

The perfect quantity is 300 ml. Enjoy this mindfully for seven days in a row. Notice the change you feel.

Eat for your metabolic health today

Can you eat for better metabolic health? Yes. It isn't just about what you eat but also how you do it and the sequence you follow. Whether you are in a hostel, on a flight, in a restaurant or on a vacation, where you do not have control over the ingredients, you can still control the flow. I call this the You Care Lifestyle Flow. Try to make these changes starting with your next meal. The sequence matters.

Thirty minutes before your meal, have one tablespoon of apple cider vinegar with mother culture mixed with a tall glass of water. Sit and sip slowly. If apple cider vinegar does not suit you, skip this step.

Steps to follow during the meal:

- First, relax. Bless your food. Give thanks and set an intention for good digestion and health.
- Then, eat your vegetables. Start with raw salads. Then move on to the cooked vegetables. As the

vegetables digest, they form a gel-like mucosal membrane that lines your intestine and slows down the absorption of carbohydrates that you eat later. If you can't eat raw foods because you have a compromised immune system or poor gut health, or have gone through colon surgery, eat the cooked vegetables first.

- Next, eat your proteins and fats.
- Lastly, eat your grains (carbohydrates).

The flow and sequence in which you eat your macros matter. You never have to be scared of eating rice if you eat it according to this flow. The problem arises when we have too much rice and not enough protein (dal) or no vegetables or eat only rice-dominant meals.

You will also have better portion control on rice/grains, which can help you lose weight, boost your energy, feel lighter, reduce stubborn fat, avoid post-meal slumps, improve blood sugar readings and boost your metabolic health.

What if you are pairing lentils or legumes with grains, for instance, rajma/kidney beans with rice or khichdi? Try to add more lentils or legumes and less grains and tubers. Here's how you can integrate it into the flow:

1. First, eat your raw salad.
2. Then, your cooked veggies.
3. Then, combine the rice or roti with dal/rajma/lentils (protein + carbs). You can eat yogurt with it too.
4. Want to eat dessert? This is the best time to eat it.

Wait! It doesn't end here.

- Avoid drinking water for at least thirty minutes after eating your food. If you must, take a few sips of water or buttermilk. Sit and sip slowly.
- Take a gentle walk for ten minutes after your meals.
- You can also sit in vajrasana (thunderbolt pose) for four to five minutes and then take a ten-minute walk if you wish.

Did you poop after waking up?

Most of us prefer to sweep our homes first thing in the morning rather than at night. Similarly, the most natural thing to do in the morning after waking up is pooping. Try to clean your bowels first thing after waking up. During your deep restorative sleep at night, your body naturally undergoes the process of detoxification. It accumulates waste products in your colon. When you wake up in the morning to natural light, your circadian rhythm or internal biological clock opens up your bowel movement. It relays a signal that you need to poop. This is the first logical step because you know that storing toxins within the body is only going to create problems. So, clean yourself inside and out first before you begin your day.

Engage in a hobby today

How many times have you mindlessly uttered a list of hobbies when someone asked you what you like to do outside your routine? I want you to reflect deeply on this today. How often do you make the time to engage in these hobbies? Studies show that hobbies boost mental alertness, concentration and self-esteem. No matter what your age, they keep you active, young and thriving at heart. They help you explore a creative outlet outside your monotonous daily routine, distract you from everyday stressors and allow you to immerse yourself in activities you enjoy.

Whether it is art and crafts, playing an instrument, board games, knitting, writing, singing, dancing, gardening or swimming—do what you like. Want to take this a step further? Involve your family members in your hobbies. Watch how simple things help strengthen lifelong bonds and build rituals and traditions you can pass down to your kids or other family members. Do this well.

Try music therapy

Have you tried chanting or singing in a group? You will instantly feel the positive vibrations, frequencies and rhythms uplifting you. Music has the power to heal. Medical science has been studying the effects of music on our overall health for a long time. And the findings are nothing short of spectacular. A scientific study concluded that music listeners have higher natural killer cells that attack infected and cancerous cells. Music improves cognitive abilities, deepens meditation, eases anxiety, promotes relaxation, boosts concentration, improves intimacy, relieves pain, uplifts mood, sharpens memory and enhances sleep. Whether it is singing, listening, chanting or playing a musical instrument—all are forms of music therapy, and you can start it right now.

It has worked amazingly well for many of my clients, and you can try it too. Enhance your health, lifestyle, happiness and joy. It could be one song or creating your own playlist, but start this therapy today.

Laugh your heart out

There is no doubt that laughter is the simplest way to keep the body and mind healthy. Do you remember how freely we would laugh our hearts out at little happenings and the most basic jokes? But as we grew older, many of us got lost in the chaos of life and forgot the simple ways to be happy. Your small win for today is to share a mirthful laugh with a loved one.

Can't think of ways to do this? Here are a few:

- Share a funny memory.
- Read a funny joke.
- Watch a comedy show or movie you love.
- Prepare a laughter list. Include the top three or four things that make you laugh when you think about them.

This simple practice can work wonders when you are having a tough day because it moves your body from the flight or fight state (sympathetic nervous system) to relaxation (parasympathetic nervous system). Laughter is a powerful drug beyond medicine. Try this today.

Go through your gallery and select a picture to reflect on

Photographs are feelings caught in motion. These evoke emotions not only when you click them, but also when you revisit them. Go through your gallery today and pick one picture to reflect on. Look at its composition and lighting. Think about the memory it stirs up in your mind. Was it a birthday, anniversary or just a mundane moment that deserved to be documented? Write down how you feel. If it is a photograph that sparks joy, observe it for at least a minute longer. Hold it close to your chest and be grateful for that moment.

Have you tried the five-minute raisin test?

Did you know a raisin can help you deepen your mindfulness practice? This is your small win for today. Try this five-minute exercise. Inspired by Buddhist teachings, legendary American professor Jon Kabat-Zinn developed this technique as part of his mindfulness-based stress reduction (MBSR). Also known as raisin meditation, many therapists and mindfulness practitioners advocate it today. This grounding exercise helps you eat mindfully and works to reduce stress.

This practice will help you enjoy a raisin like never before. Be completely present. Don't let anything distract you.

How to do it

1. Hold a raisin in your palm or between your fingers.

2. Observe its colour, ridges, folds and distinct features.

3. Feel its texture between your fingers. Close your eyes if you must.

4. Hold it close to your nose and smell it. Register the aroma.

5. Gently place the raisin in your mouth. Don't bite. Explore it with your tongue.

6. Chew the raisin slowly. Don't swallow. Let the juices flow through your palate.

7. As you experience the raisin in touch, smell and taste—swallow it. Reflect on how you feel. Do this well.

Affirm with faith and conviction

Today, practise this powerful and one of my favourite affirmations.

'Every day and in every way I am getting better and better.'

Say it with faith, belief, conviction and complete attention. Embody it as if it's already happening! Even if you do not feel good, fake it. Your mind does not know the difference between real and imagined, and this leaves you with a superpower to trick your mind and body into believing that you are getting better and better. Beliefs and thought patterns are formed through repetitions. Practise it once or a couple of times during the day.

Drop it like it's malasana!

Malasana is the most natural way to sit. Men and women in rural India still sit this way, especially while pooping. And this position makes scientific sense because it enables proper alignment for easier evacuation.

Practise malasana as a part of your morning ritual today before you visit the restroom. This pose enables a smoother and complete bowel movement and is especially useful for individuals who are constipated or complain of incomplete evacuation, flatulence and bloating. Malasana also helps open up tight hips, reduce lower back pain, strengthen glutes and feel grounded.

Hold this asana for anywhere between thirty seconds to a minute. You could even try sipping on a glass of warm water while in this pose and notice how it helps ease your bowel movements.

A mix of goodness

Nuts form an important component of balanced nutrition. Today, add a mix of raw, soaked and unsalted nuts and seeds to your food plan for a stronger and more diverse gut microbiome, improved brain health, better HDL (good cholesterol) levels, hormonal balance and muscle strength.

A mix of almonds, walnuts, pistachios, a Brazil nut (do not go overboard!) and pumpkin seeds are a great start. Make sure they are soaked well (for at least seven to eight hours) before consumption.

Please avoid these in case of nut or seed allergies/ sensitivities.

Drinking is good for your health

Water is the most powerful drink. It is medicine and even a 1 per cent drop in it can affect trillions of cells in your body. Most people think they are drinking adequate water, but when they start tracking their consumption, they realize they aren't. Summer, spring or winter, your body needs basic hydration. Even more if you are working out or sweat a lot.

Your small win today is to hydrate adequately. Aim for ten to twelve glasses of water. Set reminders or alarms if that helps. Nothing can be simpler than this!

Make your bed, transform your life

Make your bed. Yes, your own bed. Fold the blanket, tuck in the sheets, roll up the mattress, fluff the pillows. Make your bed (every day!) no matter who you are or how much help you have.

To win, we need to learn self-discipline and consistency. And it starts with small things like these. Besides that, you get to start your day with something accomplished. Even if that one task is a small thing like making your bed, it can make a world of difference to your mindset for the rest of the day.

Explore the simple pleasure of walking barefoot on the grass

Find a patch of green grass that's clear of sharp objects or debris. Take off your shoes and stand barefoot on it. Draw your attention to the soles of your feet. How do the blades of grass feel? Now start walking. Appreciate the calm and grounding effects of nature. Walk for about ten to fifteen minutes. Put your shoes back on.

Walking barefoot on a patch of green grass can provide numerous benefits for both the body and the mind. It can improve balance, posture, and strengthen the muscles in the feet and legs. Additionally, it can reduce stress and improve mood by connecting with nature and the calming effects of being surrounded by greenery. Walking barefoot on grass also increases sensory awareness by allowing you to feel the texture and temperature of the ground beneath your feet. Overall, this simple activity can be a great way to incorporate nature into your daily routine and improve your physical and mental health.

Tap into your intuition

The most important voice in this world is the voice of your inner guidance, intuition, sixth sense or whatever you may choose to call it. Your voice within always guides you on what to do and what not to do. So when you connect to the spirit within you, you are likely to find all the answers you are looking for. Your intuition is your best guide for the difficult decisions you need to make in love, relationships, work and life. And you have got to trust that instinct because that is your real voice. Everything else is either someone's advice, suggestion or perception. And only when your mind, body and spirit connect do you find intuition.

The simplest way to listen to your intuition is to sit in silence without any distractions, take a few breaths and ask the questions you have been asking the outside world. By doing this repeatedly, your inner intuition will start speaking to you.

'Good news! If you are reading this you are alive. Bad news. You don't know for how long. So, live life fully. Release that emotional baggage and past, drop grudges, forgive if you can and make the most out of your life in the best way possible.'

The gift of forgiveness

Forgiveness is difficult but necessary. There is no point in renting out your heart and mind space to someone who has hurt you. The hurt has happened. No one can ever change that. And maybe the person who hurt you has moved on too. Thus, we must learn to forgive not for the other person's wrongdoings but for ourselves—our peace and our health.

Something that can help you with forgiveness is looking back on your life and realizing how many times you have been forgiven. Most likely, several times. So if you have been forgiven, none of us hold any right not to forgive someone else. With that thought in mind, gracefully forgive someone you need to. You needn't go up to the person and say anything. Just do it in your mind and heart. Yes, it's difficult, but not impossible. The peace and lightness you will experience in your heart will be unmatched.

Here's an exercise that can help:

1. Write down the names of the people you want to forgive but are struggling to. Besides the names, write the action or injustice each person did to you (for example, hurt, betrayal, bad-mouthing and so on). As you write, you will notice clarity about your anger and the inability to forgive and a lot of strength to forgive.

2. Now, sit back, close your eyes and recentre yourself with the help of deep breaths.

3. Begin to visualize each person you are trying to forgive and imagine speaking to that person, share your true feelings with each person, and why you are hurt (go through the feelings). Have a conversation in your visualization.

4. After this, confess that you want to forgive despite finding it very difficult, because you want to move on. You will find it difficult to say this, but remember this is an illusion that you are building, and it is getting transferred to your subconscious mind.

5. Now seal this with five words—happy, healthy, abundant, loved and safe. Visualize saying:
   - *May you be happy*
   - *May you be healthy*
   - *May you be abundant*
   - *May you be loved*
   - *May you be safe*

6. Allow yourself to say this from your heart. It will come with practice, if you find it difficult.

7. Now open your eyes, go back to your list and write:

    'I have forgiven you from my heart.'
8. Tear up the paper and throw it away.
9. Use the same sequence of events for anyone you want to forgive.
10. It may not be easy for you to forgive in the first go, but repeat this exercise over and over again. It gets better with practice.

Use this technique when you need to. It is powerful and free. It may take a long time, especially if the person is living with you, but practise over and over again.

'People usually hate you for your success because it reminds them of their failures. So, succeed anyway.'

No complaints!

Habitual complaining erodes relationships, undermines success and growth, limits creativity and contributes to stress and anxiety. It's amazing how people have so much time to worry about what doesn't concern them. They have time to judge others when they have so much to fix in their own lives. So much of their time goes into comparing, judging and desiring what others have instead of staying in their lanes and focusing on how to learn, evolve and build extraordinary lives for themselves. A lot of emotional drama starts to disappear from our life when we begin to stay in our lanes and focus on ourselves and the potential we can release.

Today, Go, NoCo! Meaning, complain about nothing today, especially things you cannot control. Focus on you. Make it about you. And then, towards the end of the day, note your energy levels, happiness and satisfaction.

Anchor your affirmations

Today, anchor your affirmations with every inhale and exhale. You can make your own or use the ones shared below. Be creative, but feel it deeply as you do it. It's not your job to worry or micromanage when what you desire will happen.

On an inhale affirm
I am abundant
On an exhale affirm
I am here
On an inhale affirm
I am safe
On an exhale affirm
I am here
On an inhale affirm
I am protected
On an exhale affirm
I am here
On an inhale affirm
I receive strength

On an exhale affirm
I am here
On an inhale affirm
I am healthy
On an exhale affirm
I am here
On an inhale affirm
I create happiness
On an exhale affirm
I am here
On an inhale affirm
I am generous
On an exhale affirm
I am here
On an inhale affirm
I am guided
On an exhale affirm
I am here

You can do this in the morning, afternoon or night. That is up to you.

I like to start my day with this to anchor and ground myself. With that said, affirmations require work to be done too. So, affirm and get back to living your life and following your path with the belief that what's meant for you in your highest order will happen when it's time.

'Each time you keep complaining and whining about the same things, people or events, you are rehearsing and just rewiring your brain to get more of that and you keep building those negative neural pathways. And these get stronger and stronger as you keep rehearsing them. You know what to do. Change the amount of attention you put into those thoughts and you change and weaken those negative neural pathways and build new ones.'

Vibe higher!

You are at your lowest level of vibration when you find yourself being drawn into the negative world of blame, complaining, feelings of unworthiness, anger and bitterness. And it's easy to stay addicted to this level. Recognizing this is important because if you are vibrating low, you tend to attract everything and everyone at that level in your life. You can't desire life or a person at a higher level by staying at a lower level.

But the moment we change our level of vibration by changing our thoughts, we start elevating our vibrations and attract what is or who is at a higher level into our lives.

When our thoughts change, our feelings change too. And when our feelings change, our behaviour and experiences change as well.

Here are a few things you can do to raise your vibration almost instantly:

- Think of five things or people you are deeply grateful for.
- Go out in nature, get some sunlight and fresh air.
- Listen to two or three of your favourite songs.
- Watch something fun and laugh out loud.
- Practise a yoga flow or even one surya namaskar.
- Take a warm bath if you can.
- Light a candle.
- Do something kind for someone.
- Affirm—I am safe, I am protected, I am guided.

Do one or all of these to feel better.

'While other people's lives may look perfect on social media, remember life is what happens when it's not being recorded. Everyone is fighting a secret battle, and most won't show that part of their life on social media. So stop comparing yourself with others and start living your life and being you.'

Guilty of guilt?

Guilt is good for us. It pinches us a little so that we change our actions and behaviour, but staying stuck in chronic guilt over something we did is useless. So we instead learn, take the lesson and move on.

Guilt is a negative emotion, after all. Whenever we experience guilt, cortisol and adrenaline levels peak too. Staying stuck in guilt means having cortisol and adrenaline at an all-time high. This puts your body in a state of flight or fight or the sympathetic nervous system. As a result, your blood pressure, heart rate, blood sugar levels—everything is out of whack, and that is how we start to fall sick. There is a hormonal imbalance too, which further triggers different conditions and illnesses in our body.

Today, release that guilt within you. Take the lesson and move on.

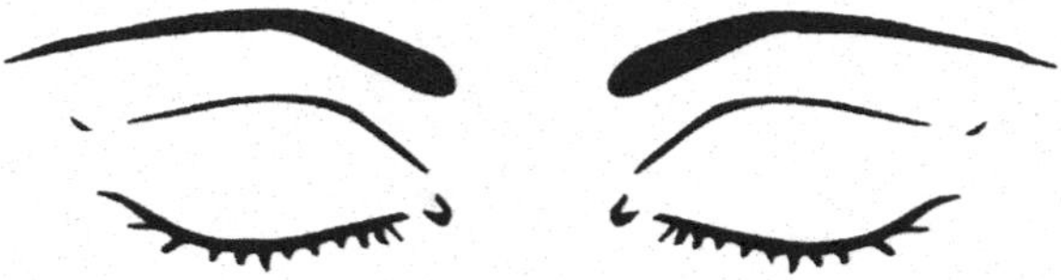

Bye-bye digital eye strain

We need our eyes for everything. It's about time we invest some time in exercising our eyes. With the extent of our exposure to screens and bright lights, we are causing degeneration of our eyes at a rapid rate. After every one to two hours of looking at your phone, laptop, tablet or television screen, stand up and look at objects that are twenty to thirty feet away (like the tip of a tree, a branch, a vase and so on) and hold your gaze for at least twenty to thirty seconds without blinking. This practice helps relieve strain and boosts eye health. And the more exposure you have to screens, the more you need to do it.

Swish your way to better dental health

Wake up, and before even sipping water or brushing your teeth, practise oil pulling for at least five minutes. Start with two minutes if you want to. You can plan to do something in those two minutes so they pass quickly. I like to sit in natural light in a malasana position as I swish the oil. I do this for five minutes, and sometimes go up to ten minutes. A regular habit of oil pulling can result in better oral microbiome, gut and teeth health and eradicates bad breath. You can use cold-pressed coconut or sesame oil for this practice. It is a simple yet powerful practice and can be part of your morning and oral hygiene routine. We are often asked why one should not gargle or swallow the oil. The simple reason is that this oil is supposed to pull toxins, bacteria, viruses and fungi out of your mouth. Gargling or swallowing the oil will push them right back into your system. So, it is best to spit it out into the sink. If you live in a cold place, it is better to spit it into your garbage to avoid clogging your drain.

This is not a replacement for brushing your teeth but meant to complement it.

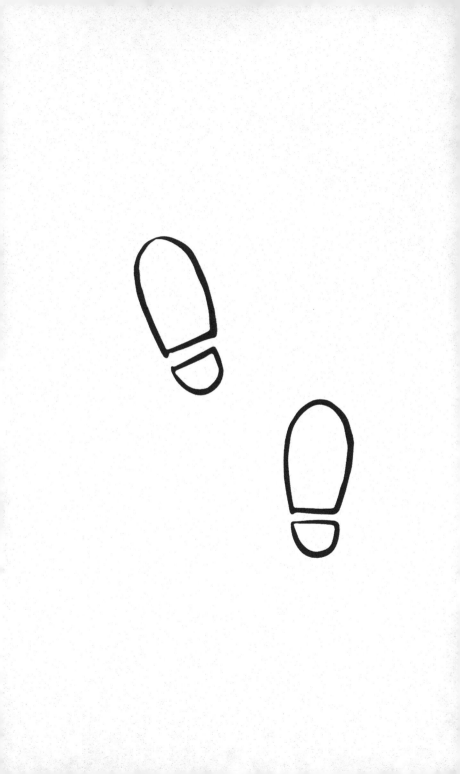

10,000 steps a day

There is no magic in 10,000 steps, but it is a good indicator of your overall activity levels in a day. Today, focus on clocking 10,000 steps (or more if you can). This is a great way to keep yourself active over and above your regimented fitness routine. If you can't manage 10,000 steps, start with 7000 or 5000 or at least 3000. Set that as a benchmark and keep adding 500 steps to that per week so you gradually reach 10,000 steps. You can use a step tracker or smartwatch to track your steps. Movement is medicine. Make it happen for you.

'If you died today, remember that your position in your organization will be replaced in maybe less than a week. Remember work–life balance and prioritize health, family relationships, love, making memories, living life and you.'

Pray, believe, surrender

Everything is energy. The food you eat, the water you drink and the air you breathe. We ourselves are a bundle of energy! We can create good or bad energy. Prayers said with a clean heart and the right intentions help generate good energy and/or change bad energy into good energy.

The three essentials when it comes to prayer are **faith, belief and surrender**. A prayer without any faith and belief is of no use. So many of us pray fervently almost daily, visit different religious places but are still anxious and worried about the very problems they prayed for. Fear takes away the goodness of every single spiritual path, and this kind of prayer holds no value. Instead, pray with utmost faith and belief and surrender the outcome. Even religion teaches us about surrendering. Above all, keep practising your prayers till you build so much faith that there isn't any room for fear anymore.

Sit down to offer prayers when you wake up or just before you go to bed tonight. Put solid belief and faith behind that prayer or the conversation you have with the high power, universe, God, providence, or whatever you want to call it, and then gracefully surrender.

Visualization is your superpower

Visualization is a powerful tool. Visualize the worst, and you get the worst. Visualize the best, and you get the best. To build great designs or perfect interiors, an architect first visualizes it, creates a design in his mind and then puts it on a piece of paper, which becomes the blueprint. The construction then begins, and a real home is created. The human mind first visualizes anything that has to be built. So, why not your health, life and personal growth?

All of us can visualize. It is a superpower we all possess. We can either use it to our advantage or disadvantage.

Sit down and visualize how you want your life, love, relationships, career and health to look. Visualize freely, without any 'ifs' and 'buts'. Visualize clearly, create a crystal-clear image and then gracefully surrender.

What do you lose by visualizing the best? Nothing. Design the life you want by using your imagination. It is beyond powerful.

Call your parents

We often get so busy growing up that we forget our parents are also growing old. If you're lucky enough to have one or both your parents alive, give them a call today. No text or email. Call them. If they stay with you, express your gratitude towards them. Find time, make time and schedule time to do this. Let them know how much they mean to you. Your time and affection are what most parents need. Time passes quickly, and it's finite. Use every moment well.

The perfect truth and lie

Every human being has a perfect truth and a perfect lie. Our perfect lie is the false stories we keep telling ourselves daily. When we stop telling ourselves that lie, we open our life, health and personal self to several possibilities of change and improvement. At the same time, all of us have our perfect truth too. Because of our low self-worth and confidence, we don't embrace the greatness and talents we own. As a result, we come in our way of shining.

The moment we overcome the perfect lie and accept the perfect truth, our life can start to change immediately: whether in a relationship, love, health, career, job or personal growth.

Sit down with yourself and acknowledge your perfect truth and lie. Realizing how we become our own obstacles is key to change.

'Remember when people try to put you down, demean you, judge you and bad-mouth you, it is the only way they know to feel better about themselves. Keep moving forward with your head up and heart bright.'

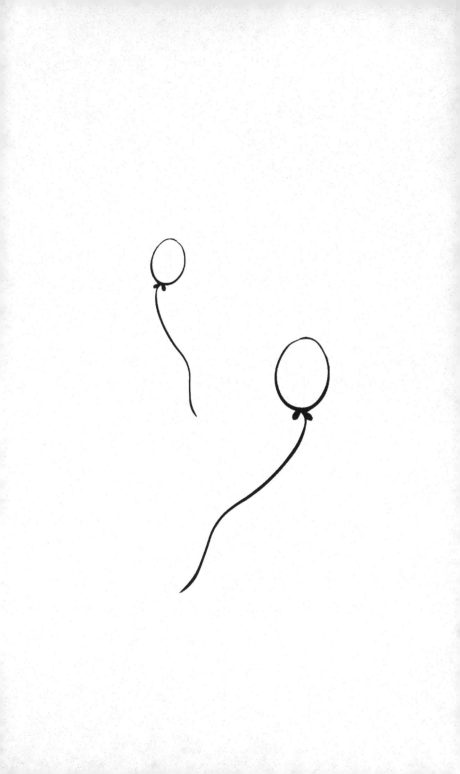

An opinion is just an opinion, not a fact

Today, try not to be attached to opinions or things people may say. This learning wasn't easy for me either. I used to say, *'I don't care what people say and think.'* But, deep down, I knew that this was just a cover-up. I did care. I am human, after all, and so are you. Accepting that enabled me to practise detachment from opinions and what people said.

With detachment, it's easy to let go and not let what others think of you become your reality. Acceptance and letting go are powerful and freeing.

Resistance, on the other hand, can feel like an obstacle.

New day, new opportunities

A new day brings new opportunities and chances to rewrite your story of how you want to live, the changes you want to make and who you want to be. The time for change is now. Not later, not tomorrow and not 1 January. When you decide enough is enough, the human mind moves towards change and action.

Today, decide and commit to that one step (no matter how small it may be) you can take to move closer to your health goal. It could be as simple as adding slices of carrots to your meal, taking a five-minute walk to a park or learning one asana.

You have one life. Live it well. Abundantly and with meaning.

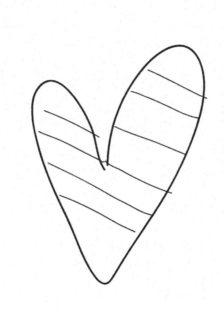

Love is the universal drug

Love is the highest and most powerful vibration of all times. That is why it feels so good to love and to be loved. The human spirit yearns to find and give love. So the most effective way to raise your vibrations is to love. When you vibrate at a higher level, you find true happiness, peace, joy, healing, great health, and you can manifest and attract.

Today, give someone your love. Make it unconditional and without expecting anything in return. It could be your partner, kid, parent or friend. Love with all your heart, in whatever way you like to—touch, a warm embrace, a conversation, making something special, a hug or kiss.

'When you don't need to compare yourself to other people, you gravitate towards things that you instinctively enjoy doing, and you are good at, and if you just focus on that for a long enough time, then chances are very high that you are going to progress and be happy.'

Be your authentic self!

Today, aim to just being the amazing and unique YOU. Too much energy and finite lifetime is wasted and depleted in trying to fit in and be someone else to please society. It's like rejecting yourself at every level. Acceptance starts with you. Accept yourself for who you are, with all your strengths and weaknesses.

There is so much power, truth and beauty in being you. You fit in just fine where you are meant to fit in, and it is effortless and joyful when it's natural!

Life moves on, and so should you

Life doesn't stop for anybody. We can wish and imagine it did, but it doesn't. This doesn't mean you can't feel the pain and that you have to be positive all the time. You can feel negativity, but what's important is how fast you choose to move from negativity to positivity.

Whenever we face pain, it is natural to feel the emotions that come with it, but then we must mindfully start the journey of moving forward and ahead.

Reflect today on where you feel stuck in life. Maybe someone has hurt you, certain life events and situations may have been unfair to you, or an incident of the past has broken you. Acknowledge the feelings but do not choose to stay broken, destroyed or hurt. Remember, time doesn't heal us. It's what we do in that time that heals. So take all the help you need but keep moving ahead.

'Most of us see rejection as a form of defeat, humiliation and failure. There is another way to view it. Accepting rejection as a form of protection and guidance allows you to flow with life and come out of difficult and negative feelings when rejected. Trust there is something/someone better meant for you. Drop your fear of rejection.'

Rejection is divine redirection

Through my years of experience, I have learnt to see rejection as a form of protection. It all comes with trusting that when something or someone doesn't work out the way it was planned for me, it's because there is something or someone far better and greater in store for me.

If you get turned down on a date or in love, it's because there is someone else better for you, or if you don't get that job, it's because there is something better for you. Trust, don't resist.

Today, spend some time reflecting on your past, where you have experienced rejection. It could be in a job, business, relationship, academics or social circle. Most of the time, you might feel grateful to be where you are today.

See rejection as a form of protection and guidance. Yes, it sounds difficult, but difficult doesn't mean impossible. The more we try with an open mind and heart, the more we are open to seeing and learning. Practise well.

Blessing or a lesson?

Bitter things happen. Better experiences happen. That's life. We can either entangle ourselves in this, become victims of our past or be stuck in 'Why me?' mode, which does nothing but create more bitterness in our minds and hearts. Or, we can try to see things from a different light and consider every person or incident in our life as a blessing or lesson.

Everything in life has a meaning and purpose. Nothing happens by accident regardless of whether it's a positive or negative incident.

Too many people today are stuck in the past. Considering your past as your blessing or lesson makes it easier for us to move forward.

'Your luxury car and branded clothes in no way define your self-worth. Have them if you can truly afford them and your intention is comfort. If your intention is validation and acceptance, you know your low self-worth is driving you and you need to fix it, brands certainly won't.'

Express to someone you love

Today, reflect on the people you truly love. Remember and pray for them. Send them beautiful energy, an email, a note, a word, an emoji or a message. Let them know how loved they are by you, and then embrace what you feel in your heart. It's a beautiful feeling.

Go sunset to sunrise

Today, try to finish your dinner by sunset, and don't eat until the sun rises the next day. This is called circadian fasting and is a small win towards aligning with the laws of nature. Sunset to sunrise is a sacred time. Every single cell of our body works according to a rhythm. The more aligned it is with the rhythm of nature, the healthier we are. If you can, try this for a week: stop eating after sunset and only eat your first meal after sunrise. That's about twelve hours of beautiful circadian rhythm fasting. Do this consistently for one to two weeks and you will never go back to your previous lifestyle.

Rejection in mind is rejection in the body

We need to understand the power of our subconscious mind. If you are on pills or medication and you take them thinking, 'Oh! This pill is dangerous. It has side effects, and it will make me feel horrible', then your mind has already rejected it. Rejection in mind is rejection in the body at a cellular level. At the same time, acceptance in mind means acceptance at a physical level in the human body.

Whether it's a medicine, treatment, chemotherapy session or food item, accept it in your mind first. Then, affirm that you will be absolutely fine with it. Move from rejection to acceptance today.

Three-finger gratitude exercise

We all know that gratitude is a powerful drug. This gratitude exercise is called the three-finger gratitude, and it helps us to be in a state of gratitude throughout the day. Here's what you need to do: Every three hours, pause, take a few deep breaths and remind yourself of three things that happened in the last three hours that make you feel grateful. It could involve people too. You can do this several times a day. Start with at least once. This also helps train your mind to look for things that are going well for you.

'Easy come, easy go
Easy sex? Loses its value
Easy money? Loses its value
Easy fad weight loss? Loses its value and comes back
Easy short-cuts building a business? Loses its value and
eventually the business
A good life is inclusive of sacrifice, hard work, effort,
discipline and consistency.'

Know your life values

What are your core life values? What are your absolute essentials in life to make it a fulfilling and meaningful one? Understanding your own life values can help you determine what is most important to you. They form a central part of who you are and who you want to be. It is only when you know your values that you can align your actions to them. This is key to living a happy and authentic life. Otherwise, we just become puppets to society and do what others say because we do not know what we want.

Today, your small win is to sit down, recentre yourself with a few deep breaths and list down your top five life values (not in any particular order).

Some examples of life values are honesty, discipline, health, freedom, punctuality, happiness and so on.

Stop slouching!

Your posture is not just for aesthetics, it determines your health at every level. Right from your spine, back and neck health to breathing capacity, confidence levels and self-esteem, your posture plays a crucial role. Every inch we stoop forward while glued to our screens adds more and more weight to our spine, which is designed to carry only a specific amount of weight. Bad posture also compresses bones and joints, inhibits muscle fibre growth and leads to reduced strength or stature.

Win today by being mindful of your posture and correcting it several times in a day. Whether you are sitting or standing, straighten that back, lengthen the spine, tuck your tailbone in, roll your shoulders back, tuck your chin in, relax your jaws and keep a gentle smile on your face. As you improve your posture, notice the boost in your confidence levels and the way you carry yourself.

Four minutes to massive transformation

Whether it's your health, relationships or any other aspect of your life that involves negative emotions and struggles, the four-minute rule will help you move forward. This addresses your emotional health because today even science is proving the impact of emotions on our physical health. Everything starts with a thought. Your thoughts become feelings, feelings become emotions, emotions dictate your behaviour, and your behaviour becomes your experience.

So, how do you address this if your mind has more negative thoughts than positive ones? This four-minute rule will help, and it is simple.

You have only four minutes in a day to complain, blame, whine and victimize yourself. After those four minutes, snap out of that zone and move to action.

For example, someone said something negative about you or things didn't go your way. Now, you have only four minutes to be angry, put yourself into 'why me' mode, complain and be as negative as you want to be. But from the fifth minute, move to action, because the only way to make a change is to action what you need to. Putting a full stop to your blaming and whining is important because it is easy for these emotions to consume you. And in this process, the only one losing is yourself.

All of us are going to go through negative emotions. Go through them, but do not become a slave to them. All you have is four minutes.

Eat a carrot before your meal today

What if there was one thing you could do every day to help boost eye, hormonal and gut health, prevent fungal and bacterial infections, assist fat loss and prevent cancer or support its management? It's not a special diet or an expensive supplement. It's a humble veggie hiding in plain sight. Fully grown and raw carrots! The research on carrots for their ability to prevent cancer progression, heal fungal infections, lower oestrogen levels, balance hormones, boost vision and assist fat loss is revolutionary. Carrots contain falcarinol, which has been scientifically studied for its role in cancer prevention by slowing down the progression of cancer cells and supporting cell apoptosis. Besides that, carrots also contain a unique indigestible fibre that helps sweep away excess oestrogen from the body as we poop, thereby preventing or reducing oestrogen dominance, which is the root cause of most hormone-dependent cancers, PCOD, infertility and man boobs.

Just slice a raw carrot and try to consume it before your lunch and dinner, or at least one meal. Pack it for your kid's tiffin or snack box too. Make it a culture in your family to eat a carrot before meals, unless you are allergic to them.

Wake up to a few bed stretches

Before you get out of bed every morning, or even before you sleep, try to get some bed stretches in. Simple yoga poses such as *child's pose, cobra pose* and *reclining twists* can go a long way in boosting blood circulation, combating stiffness, stretching your back, opening up the pelvic region and making you feel recharged for the rest of the day. And guess what? You also end up stoking your metabolic activity.

This is especially necessary if you have very cushiony mattresses because they tend to slowly ruin our back as they aren't natural to us. Hold each pose for about thirty to forty-five seconds, take slow deep breaths and get going with your day!

Move to action . . . MTA

You can keep talking and complaining about your sickness, misfortunes, who wronged you and your losses. But, once it is done, put a full stop to it and take some action. The more you discuss all the negativities in your life, the more they become your truth. Stop remaining stuck because it does nothing to make you feel better. Instead, talk about happiness and things that are going well for you. The more you talk about the goodness in your life, the more it becomes your truth.

Whenever you feel sad, low and negative, dive straight into your mind and see what thoughts you are rehearsing and repeatedly saying because just by saying them again and again, you are creating your suffering. And only you can break this pattern. No drugs, alcohol or medicines can. Only you. Take that responsibility instead of outsourcing it to someone else. Yes, share, vent and take all the help you need, but only you can break the cycle and move to action. With anything, there is always an action to be taken, and excuses are little justifications for feeling better and validating our non-doing.

Do this today. Sometimes we have to suck it up and do it. It may be difficult, but difficult doesn't mean impossible.

Consistency over intensity

Never forget the power of consistency and its compounding effect. If you want to get better at meditation, practice and consistency are the only way to achieve this. Today, if you sit down to meditate for three minutes, practise until you can sit for four minutes, then five minutes and so on. That is how to build up your practice slowly.

Too many people think that you must meditate for thirty minutes or an hour for it to be successful. But, who said that? Meditating for two minutes is successful too because you showed up and tried. So now, you only have to do it over and over again. Nothing is easy, but it gets better with practice and consistency. Win at consistency today.

What grace did you receive today?

Every day and every moment of our lives, we are receiving something. It's when we are mindful and living with consciousness that we are able to see and feel the grace we receive every day in so many ways. It could be a kind gesture of your colleague, the warm embrace of your partner or simply realizing that you got another day to live. Today, sit down peacefully and reflect on what grace you received and in what form.

Savasana—the deep yogic rest

A beautiful, simple, powerful yet free technique that originated in ancient India and can help you transition into a state of deep relaxation, rejuvenation, improved blood circulation, concentration, sleep, calmness and balanced blood pressure is savasana or corpse pose. This pose allows you to relax after your yoga session. Here, while your body is static and relaxed, your mind is inwardly active, and you sequentially relax every part of your body from toes to head as you breathe in and out from your belly and gradually melt into the ground. Whether you practice yoga or not, are in a hotel room or in your home, you can still get into savasana. This is great for people who are chronically sleep deprived, anxious, depressed, mentally or physically fatigued.

How to do it

1. Lie flat on your back. Use a small pillow below your neck if absolutely required. Close your eyes.

2. Keep your legs at a comfortable distance apart and let your feet and knees relax completely, toes facing opposite sides.

3. Place your arms alongside your body. Leave your palms open to the sky and fingers softly curled.

4. Taking your attention to different parts of your body one by one, slowly relax your entire body.

5. Begin with bringing your awareness to your right foot, move on to your right knee, then right thigh (as you complete one leg, move your attention to the other leg) and so on, and slowly move upwards to your head, relaxing each part of the body.

6. Keep breathing slowly, gently, deeply, and allow your breath to relax you more and more. The incoming breath energizes the body while the outgoing breath brings relaxation. Drop all sense of hurry or urgency or any need to attend to anything else. Just be with your body and your breath. Surrender your whole body to the floor and let go.

7. After some time, about ten to twenty minutes, when you feel fully relaxed, keeping your eyes closed, slowly roll on to your right side. Lie in that position for a minute or so. Then, taking the support of your right hand, gently sit up and assume a seated pose such as sukhasana or the simple cross-legged pose.

8. Keep your eyes closed and take a few deep breaths as you gradually become aware of your environment and body. When you feel complete, slowly and gently open your eyes.

'When your understanding of wealth goes beyond just your bank balance and includes love, memories, deep relationships, deep connections and personal luxuries like the freedom to choose, accept, let go, and time, you are awakening.'

Juggle your way to a sharper and smarter brain

Juggling is not just a circus skill. It is a scientifically proven brain sharpening skill, and who doesn't want a sharp and smart brain? All you need to do is get two balls and start juggling. By doing this, you strengthen the white and grey matter in your brain, the two most important aspects of brain health and cognitive abilities. The grey matter involves processing of thoughts, emotions, memory retention, learning, grasping power and thinking, and the white matter allows communication between two grey matter areas. When it starts to degenerate, we experience memory loss issues.

Even if you're not perfect at juggling and drop the ball several times, it is okay. You are still strengthening your brain in several ways.

It's a fantastic activity for those experiencing forgetfulness, memory loss, inability to concentrate or even to prevent degenerative conditions such as Alzheimer's, Parkinson's and dementia. It also helps improve the hand-eye-brain coordination.

Give the candle a meditative stare

With stress, fear and uncertainty all around us, anything that can induce a relaxation response is worth giving a try. Today, light a candle or a diya and stare at the flame for as long as you can without blinking your eyes. If tears roll down your cheeks, allow them to, but in doing so not only do you calm your racing mind, but also cleanse your eyes, improve focus and concentration, and cultivate peace in your mind and heart. This is an ancient yogic practice and is also called trataka.

How to do it

1. Sit in either padmasana (lotus pose) or sukhasana (easy pose), extend the spine and relax the body.
2. Place a candle about two feet in front of you at eye level.
3. Make sure your surroundings are quiet and not too bright with either natural or artificial light.

4. Calm the mind. Close your eyes for about six breaths before you start the practice of trataka.

5. Fix your gaze by staring at the centre of the burning candle, the tip of the wick.

6. Do not blink while staring at the flame.

7. Continue gazing at the candle till your eyes feel the need to blink or until they begin to water.

8. Close your eyes, but continue to visualize the flame. The space between the two eyebrows, or the third eye, is the point at which this image should be visualized.

9. Repeat this for two to three rounds, then relax completely with eyes closed to end the practice of trataka.

10. Rub your hands together and generate heat. Now cup your palms over your eyes for relaxation.

Clear the clutter

Walk into your bedroom. Open the cupboards and drawers and start removing anything that you haven't used in the last six months. Donate or give away what you can, and dump what you should. You will be surprised to see how much of what you have accumulated isn't really needed. This is called decluttering. This simple activity makes you feel light and is great for your emotional and mental wellness. Start with one room and then slowly declutter your entire home.

Scrape your tongue

The simple act of scraping your tongue every morning after brushing your teeth can go a long way in improving your oral hygiene and health, which is everything for holistic health. It helps remove harmful bacteria that can inflame your gums as well as cause cavities. A cleaner tongue also gets rid of bad breath and improves the sense of taste.

We have encouraged patients who had COVID-19 and lost their sense of taste to do this and it worked well for many. Opt for using a copper or steel scraper rather than a plastic one, and don't scrape too hard, else you will damage your taste buds temporarily.

Karma comes back to bite you
If you are blessed with a great body, don't use it to make others feel inferior about themselves. Karma comes back to bite you and you ain't gonna like it!
If you have wealth, don't use arrogance and dominance over others who may not have it. Karma comes back to bite you and you ain't gonna like it!

If you have designation and power, don't use it to dominate or control others. You may lead but don't be arrogant!
Live simply yet abundantly. Strive to be humble.

Remember karma.

Did you take a mindful shower today?

Everyone who loves a good shower can vouch for the fact that these are therapeutic. A powerful way to improve this experience is to do it more mindfully. Don't merely jet your way through it. Let the distractions go and use this time to focus solely on YOU. Reflect on how you think and feel with every step. Observe how your thoughts change.

How to do it

- Listen to the sound of the water hitting the floor. Slowly step into the shower.
- Feel every drop of water touching your head and cascading down your body.
- Notice the temperature, the rhythmic flow and the droplets on your skin.
- Soap your body and breathe in its fragrance.

- Remind yourself how precious your body is as you scrub it gently.
- Take ten deep breaths and relax.
- Once done, rinse your body slowly.
- Visualize yourself washing away your anxieties, sadness and worries.
- Watch the negative thoughts flow down the drain.
- Reflect on how you feel. Offer gratitude for a clean body.

'Be you. Don't waste a lifetime trying to be someone else. You can never be someone else. Be you and let those around you adjust. The right will stay, the wrong will go, for your own good.'

The art of doing nothing

The French call it *l'art de ne rien faire*. It refers to the sweetness of doing nothing. Pick a day, take a break and do nothing. Don't attach any guilt to it. Find joy in it. You may be conditioned to think that you have to be on your toes in this 'always-on' world. But that's not true. Sometimes all you need to do is slow down. You don't have to be productive 24x7. Honour your body and your time off. Allow yourself to recuperate and rejuvenate without setting any expectations. Do this well. But don't let yourself go mindlessly. Write down how the art of doing nothing feels.

Smell something wonderful today

How often do you pause and smell the roses? Or anything that makes you happy? Your small win for today is to awaken one of your best senses—the sense of smell. Be it coffee beans, tea leaves, a flower or perfume, mindfully close your eyes and breathe it in.

Ask yourself:

What do you feel?
How does your mood change?
What sensations do you go through?
Do any memories come up?

Your sense of smell is a power that connects experience with memories and moments.
Practise this well today.

'People who are involved in gossip about others and spreading rumours are the ones with the most boring, empty, lifeless lives. It is why they need entertainment to be created in their lives through these shallow ways. Be so busy building an extraordinary life for yourself that you rise.'

A parting note to you

Dear readers,

Thank you for taking the time out to read this labour of love. Maybe one or many of these small wins inspired you. Now all you need to do is be consistent with them. Start with one win and do it every day until you no longer have to remind yourself to do it because it has become part of your lifestyle. Do what suits you. Build a culture of small wins within your family and relationships. It's always great to do these as a team. It makes others feel involved, and you have accountability buddies. It is inspiring and motivating too. Take one small win every week as a family goal, and reward yourselves when you have done it consistently for a week.

These small wins are some of the most powerful among the many that we have been using in our practice with clients around the globe for years. There are many more that will come out soon in a new book. Hopefully, by then, you will all be experts at most of the small wins in this book.

With love and gratitude,
Luke

Gratitude and thanks

This book is a labour of love and a tribute to the resilient human spirit that believes every win, no matter how small, is worth celebrating. It wouldn't have been possible without the support of many people.

My gratitude and thanks to my family, clients and patients across the globe who inspire me through their journeys and our journeys with them to keep learning and evolving our practice backed by science, research, and life experiences.

To Taarika, who has worked with me on previous books and now this. And Jovita, who has been part of this book, her first time with me. To Vaishali, our head of design, and her student Stuti Shah for the beautiful hand-drawn illustrations. To Milee, with whom we have had a great relationship that continues to grow in the field of books and knowledge.

To Team Luke, my backbone, for the incredible work we do every single day and for keeping our vision alive. And immense gratitude to all our fans, followers and patients around the world, who not only believed but followed and practised each of these small wins over the years with discipline and consistency. The exceptional results they encountered in different spheres of their lives and the powerful testimonials that poured in were reassurance of the power of small wins and the science behind them. It inspired us to write this book and present it to the world.

What is the You Care Wellness Programme all about?

The You Care Wellness Programme (YWP) is a holistic, integrative medicine and lifestyle programme designed around YOU. It revolves around your condition, medication, goals, the nutrition you need, integrated with movement and exercise guidance, sleep, and empowering you with the tools to build sound emotional health and wellness.

YWP recognizes and respects all forms of medicine and is not alternative medicine. Yes, there is a massive focus on managing the side effects of any medication you may be on and using an integrative lifestyle to help you slowly reduce or get off your medication under the supervision of your doctor and our team. But this programme goes beyond and helps you plan a personalized approach towards a healthier YOU.

The programme revolves around five pillars designed around the unique and special YOU—deep and intelligent cellular nutrition, adequate movement and exercise, quality sleep, emotional detox and wellness, and the spirit. These are the foundational platforms for prevention and recovery in integrative and lifestyle medicine.

The You Care Wellness Programme respects your uniqueness and works with the understanding that no one size fits all. Every programme and journey is personalized according to your past or present lifestyle, health condition, symptoms and root causes. Integrative and lifestyle medicine focuses on addressing the root cause of the problem and works to manage the side effects of medications and treatments that may cause secondary problems, issues and discomfort. While symptoms are being treated, root causes must be addressed, and rebuilding with a focus on future prevention is important. Every disease requires this approach, from a simple case of acne to a rare syndrome or cancer.

On this journey with us, a team of highly skilled nutritionists, clinical dietitians, allopathic doctors, yoga therapists, life coaches and certified emotional counsellors will be assigned to your case according to the condition and if required. Medical doctors trained in integrative and lifestyle medicine over and above their medical qualifications oversee the programme and dietary plans. All these experts come together to form an integrative team that will help you find a way on your journey to wellness and a healthier YOU.

Our protocols for every medical condition or problem you come to us with, revolve around these fundamental intelligent systems within the human body involved in prevention, recovery and rebuilding.

1. The microbiome (gut)
2. Immunity and inflammation
3. DNA repair
4. Stem cell regeneration
5. Angiogenesis and antiangiogenesis
6. Sleep

Our programmes in no way guarantee you a cure or miraculous healing. We will never sell you anything in that light. We believe in a structured approach, knowledge, research, wisdom and years of experience to assess you and your condition as unique and plan your protocol on those lines.

A cure may not be possible for some illnesses, but we firmly believe there is always room for healing. Healing can be experienced as acceptance of illness and peace with one's life. This healing is spiritual at its core and can involve learning to live with a condition and improving other parts of your health—physical, emotional and spiritual. It can include improving the quality of your life by empowering yourself with the right lifestyle, food, movement and tools to enable emotional wellness and the spirit.

We are not a replacement for your medical team and will never suggest otherwise unless we feel that your current medical approach is ineffective and dangerous to you. We put care, love, respect and understanding in our approach and design healthcare around the person first and then the disease. It is our commitment to simplifying health and lifestyle. To make wellness enjoyable and wonderful, instead of horrible.

We commit our best to everyone who comes to us. And while we cannot always promise the end results, we always promise to be there for you and give our all to you, your family and loved ones. Our only hope for you is to get better and live a happier and healthier life.

Team Luke welcomes you to an inward journey towards better health, acceptance, love and unlocking inner healing power and peace. Become a force of healing for yourself, in your families, communities, relationships and this one beautiful life you have.

We help you find a way.

Get in touch with us

Visit our website: www.lukecoutinho.com
Call: 1800 102 0253
WhatsApp us: +91 98207 20253
Email: info@lukecoutinho.com
Instagram: @luke_coutinho
Facebook: @LukeCoutinhoOfficial
Twitter: @LukeCoutinho17
LinkedIn: Luke Coutinho
YouTube: Luke Coutinho

How small wins every day have transformed thousands of lives

Top commenter
Sabita Challinger

Where do I start? Dr Luke I was 94 kgs n depressed n feeling sorry for myself due to declining health n 50%of physical disability. But since I have been watching your videos n suggestions.. I decided to give myself a challenge. I bought a smaller plate divided into sections larger side for Vegetables. Smaller space for Carbs n in between for Protein. Gradually I have learnt n understood n assimilate all suggestions you give in your videos. Small win leads to bigger win. I now weigh 84 kgs. Started to attend Wellbeing Hub practising yoga. Easier to get on mat. But getting up after relaxation I am like a contorsonist. Need props. Prosthetic knees refuse to move.

I felt guilty n carried a heavy burden since I was 10 was molested by a close member of the family. It was taboo to talk about this mentally damaging time of my childhood. But watching your video on keeping guilt n blaming oneself. Help to ease my guilt n anger. I could not understand why would an adult abuse an innocent child

N still pretend to be a kind person.

I have managed to overcome this in my light years.

I owe you big time. Respect to you Dr for your generous support. I may be just a number to you But You have been my Saviour. I am not Ashamed anymore.

I took heed of all your talks. Watched your

Hi Luke sir, just completed my first half marathon at 42 today and would like to share this small win and thanks to you for the simplicity of the magic recipe of your home made electrolyte with rock salt, lemon and and water. As you say that simplicity is the new luxury this year for 2023.
Thanks to you again Sir 🙏
Will keep coming back with small wins with your holistic lifestyle solutions

Tushar Pradhan
Cover 2 is standout for me. From Darkness to light. Same goes with small wins to great wins of life. My small wins are my routine habits with consistency over intensity. A little progress each day in health, food, excercises is building a resilient person in me ready to take up the difficult challenges of life. Gratitude, Humbleness, meticulous efforts in right direction is path of terrefic transformation..... being the stunning version of your ownself is the key..... remmember there is no competition with other its only with you trying to be your own better version each day....!!

___kkabss___ 1w

Cover 2, which is happy and colorful.

#Smallwins have changed my life. I have a huge list, but to name a few: (1) Sleeping by 10pm and waking up early without any alarm. (2) IntermittentFasting since 2017 and the countless and effortless benefits that come with it. I even got a compliment from Luke himself, he said I've maintained myself very well. IF comes naturally to me, like breathing. (3) Completing more than 10,000+ steps every single day, including weekends and holidays. (4) OilPulling has improved my gum health and my teeth have become whiter than ever before. Thank you Luke! 🤍😊🙌

5 likes   Reply   Message

smallwins_with_luke_coutinho 1w

We are excited to see the responses. Keep them coming 🙌 🤍

6 likes   Reply   Message

siddharthrajsekar ✓ 4d

White

2 likes   Reply   Message

devigorasia 1w

Both covers are beautiful very thoughtfully designed . My small wins have been to practice gratitude every morning and evening it brings a huge shift to the day.

3 likes   Reply   Message

nishasachdevabathla 1w

I will go with the blue 🤍

1 like   Reply   Message

vezzozahra 1w

1) After following you i started thinking about myself. I started following and owning my soul n body. 2) firstly i started enjoying my meal with gratitude and seeing my food in new way. 3)morning stretch, early morning sun light on bike with husband. Which i never noticed before. 4) nutmeg oil. 5)i started enjoying and celebrating small thing. 6)vegas nerve 7)20-20-20-20.8) started noticing power of nature. 9)intermittent fasting. I didn't lose weight but my body is getting shape.10) power of sleep. And listtt goess on.

8 likes   Reply   Message

shirin_shaikh29 1w

Cover - 2, visually appealing and striking.

Small win - Being grateful for each new day, this sense of gratitude keeps one happy and content all day 🙏

2 likes　　Reply　　Message

kirandesetty 1w

The white cover 👌.

My small wins:

1) Enjoy 30-35 mins of lifting weights daily. Realised I was skipping and having long breaks from the gym when targeting long sessions.

2) Switching off gadgets while eating and chewing slowly and mindfully.

3) Diabetic who couldn't let go of my idlis & dosas, so have them made of millets now (Thanks to mum)

4) Trying hard but unable to do meditation for more than a few mins. So instead I do mindful deep breaths watching sunsets daily on the rooftop. 🌆 This has immensely helped in giving me clarity whats the real 'richness' in life.

The first desired result in just a month is that my borderline BP readings look in range now. 😄

4 likes　　Reply　　Message

⬦ Top fan
Alpana Baruah
My choice is Cover #2. You have been a great inspiration in my life. I was in a pretty bad shape especially emotionally last year after I had lost my job. You had come as a ray of hope and light in my life. I have learnt a lot of things from you. I have many small wins which has positively impacted my life. Currently I am also taking part in the jumping jacks challenge for 5 days and hope to continue it for rest of my life. Following N.E.A.T has helped me lose a lot of fat. Including one carrot everday to my lunch has improved my eyesight. There are too many things and I can go on and on. You are my role model whom I look upto everday. You are a blessing for me. Thank you Luke. 😊😊🖤🖤👏👏 👏👏🙏🙏

💬 Top commenter
Abigail Miranda
At first glance, Cover 2 appealed to me more than Cover 1. Enjoy watching Luke's 1.30 show on Facebook, though as a recording coz I am teaching in school during the day. Try to implement some of the valuable tips given. Small wins for me.

1 w   Like   Reply   🗨💟 · 1 💟

✏ **Author**
Luke Coutinho ✓
Abigail Miranda 😊🙏

🗨 Top commenter
Seema Ramakrishnan
Cover 2...Small wins ...ohhh there are many...
affirmations have made a vast difference in how
I look at life and how it has helped me as an
individual to lead an awesome life...life is simple
and completely in our hands how we can make it
a best version we have ever lived..thanks Luke
for always guiding us with ur simple techniques
and ur guidance has always been there to
support us whenever we look for an answer 🤍
🤍 🤍

🗨 Top commenter
Sangeeta Varyani
Cover1.

I have actually experienced the small wins.
As I was going through my chemo and enrolled
under the cancer care program of Luke Coutinho
I was unable to sleep. a small suggestion like
writing my days activities helped me to sleep
better. I will call it a BIG WIN. So simple yet
powerful. Gratitude 😊

💬 **Top commenter**
Ramya Rajesh
Both look good but cover 1 with the white background looks cleaner and catches the eye! #smallwins pranayama was intimidating for me at first. But after following you and then joining your program, I started small and now practice every single day for minimum 10 minutes. I feel so much calmer, my breathing seems so much fuller and simpler and it is helping with other side effects I have from medical treatment.

nishah1 1w
Love the white cover.. small wins helps me stay motivated... sun shine first thing in the morning has fixed my circadian cycle .. movement through the day has helped me reduce a lot of body pain due to stiffness !! Small wins are actually big wins.. 🤍🤍

kirandesetty 1w
The white cover 👌 .
My small wins:
1) Enjoy 30-35 mins of lifting weights daily. Realised I was skipping and having long breaks from the gym when targeting long sessions.
2) Switching off gadgets while eating and chewing slowly and mindfully.
3) Diabetic who couldn't let go of my idlis & dosas, so have them made of millets now (Thanks to mum)
4) Trying hard but unable to do meditation for more than a few mins. So instead I do mindful deep breaths watching sunsets daily on the rooftop. 🌆 This has immensely helped in giving me clarity whats the real 'richness' in life.
The first desired result in just a month is that my borderline BP readings look in range now. 😄

2 likes   Reply

anjali.rajpal18 1w

I have been able to completely cure my chronic anxiety, depression, high BP, rapid heartbeat, motion sickness and thin hairline problems by doing small wins everyday, over a course of few years

shirazmedhora 1w

The first cover, white brings brightness n positivity. Oh I owe my mental n physical progress to you completely, Sir. My small wins, early dinner, cold pressed oils, oil pulling, MTA, thank u for everything.

nitisharda 1w

Cover 2 My small wins all inspired by you !!!
Intermittent fasting -eating as per circadian rhythm , regular exercise, adequate sleep. Like you always say- getting the fundamentals right 😂 !!

mohata.nikita 1w

Cover 1, Luke Sir.

My small wins : 1) following circadian rhythm

2) intermittent fasting for 12-13 hours.

3) 10k steps 5-6 days a week

4) rainbow colours on food plate

5) avoiding gluten and diary for 5 days after every few weeks

6) trying to take sunshine everyday

Thank you for all your videos that share with us abundant knowledge

Asha D'sa

Cover 1.

Congrats Luke and love to have this in my collection and I am also going to gift a copy to my kids...

Following you has been a great blessing.. Immensely grateful to you for sharing the knowledge to enhance our lives..

I have always been a very disciplined person when it comes to eating..

But giving up sugar, intermittent fasting, dinner at sunset... Movement.. Breathing techniques for good sleep.. These have made a lot of difference to me..

I never miss going through ur post whenever I open my fb or Insta.. I have cut down my phone time.. Avoid phone time before bed and after rising Its a small win too...

Small wins every day has been my slogan now.. My conversations with my kids end with this line...

May this book come as a light to many more who need it 🙏🙏

soni_musicbuff 1w

'Small wins' and 'Move to action ' , these two catch phrases are so deeply embedded in my brain now ! Thanks to Luke . My everyday aim is to keep the sugars to minimum and move as much as I can . And if I falter, to be kind to self and spring back to action . All this are so profound and life changing . Thanks A ton ! 🙏

doctor__of_sweetpills 1w

Hai Luke Sir 😊 First of all heartfully Thank you so much for inspiring us every day with ur concept of small wins 😍 When I open my insta i search for ur posts and check on ur stories first to learn the new things which we are barely using in our day to day life!!! In this busy world we are too busy in pleasing PPL but not focusing on ourselves our own inner self,You have made us to realise simplicity is new luxury and that deep slow breathing took my breath away 😂😂 Becoz till date I dint see PPL talking about this kind of Small yet most imp thing to our Life 🐌 Bless you abundantly with so much pH (peace & happiness 😌)

jmariefernz I am winning in life, Amen 🖤🙌🔥

43w   1 like   Reply   Send

 sangeetha.duruvasan I love how you say , ' Try again'! Truly - small wins 🔥

5d   1 like   Reply   Send

 lakshmisharath Consistency is everything . That's been my motto for the last couple of months and focussing on small wins

5d   Reply   Send

 seema_singh_2b The word you say "small wins " .... really means a lot

7w   1 like   Reply   Send

 sampoornposhan Small wins makes bigger change in so many people life's Thankyou so much @luke_coutinho

7w   1 like   Reply   Send

 renu0710 I am winning everyday...happy rather elated...I cleared clutter almost 5 days daily...donated..thanks Luke .. gratitude..u motivate me terribly

2w   Reply   Send

 arjun.divgi These little snippets about holistic and integrative lifestyle has really helped transform my approach towards fitness, into one that's fun, realistic and sustainable 💪 ! @luke_coutinho

43w   📌 Pinned   5 likes   Reply   Send

 luke_coutinho ✅ @arjun.divgi keep winning

43w   1 like   Reply   Send

shalsoman Mindful eating is my goal for the year and consciously making it a habit.... Small wins indeed 🙏🦶

43w   Reply   Send

 vaibhav_lokare_ Step by step Little bit winning .... 🙌 🖤

43w   2 likes   Reply   Send